Meaningful Brain

Imagination and the Meaningful Brain

Arnold H. Modell

A Bradford Book
The MIT Press
Cambridge, Massachusetts
London, England

First MIT Press paperback edition, 2006

MIT Press books may be purchased at special quantity discounts for business or sales promotional use. For information, please email special_sales@mitpress.mit.edu or write to Special Sales Department, The MIT Press, 55 Hayward Street, Cambridge, MA 02142.

This book was set in Palatino by Achorn Graphic Services, Inc., and was printed and bound in the United States of America.

Library of Congress Cataloging-in-Publication Data

Modell, Arnold H., 1924–
Imagination and the meaningful brain / Arnold H. Modell.
    p.   cm.
Includes bibliographical references and index.
ISBN-10: 0-262-13425-X (hc : alk. paper) – 0-262-63343-4 (pb : alk. paper)
ISBN-13: 978-0-262-13425-5 (hc : alk. paper) – 978-0-262-63343-7 (pb : alk. paper)
1. Imagination. 2. Meaning (Psychology). 3. Emotions and cognition. 4. Mind and body. I. Title.
BF408. M58   2003
150.19'5—dc21
                                                              2002029595

10   9   8   7   6   5   4   3

For Lora

What is most human is not rationalism but the uncontrolled and incontrollable continuous surge of creative radical imagination in and through the flux of representation, affects and desires.

Cornelius Castoriadis

Contents

Preface

The basic premise that informs this book is that *human experience cannot be omitted from a scientific explanation of how the mind/brain works.* The intrapsychic complexities of human psychology, as observed through introspection and the empathic knowledge of other minds, must be added to the third-person perspective of cognitive psychology and neuroscience. As a psychoanalyst, this is what I have attempted to do.

My interest in neuroscience was stimulated by a completely fortuitous encounter with Gerald Edelman's book *Neural Darwinism,* which described his theory of neuronal group selection. I was attracted to his selectionist viewpoint and his global theory of the mind/brain, which seamlessly moved between neural and mental concepts. More specifically, I was excited to discover that Edelman's view of memory as a recategorization is very similar to a theory of memory that Freud had proposed in 1896 and unfortunately later ignored. I subsequently made use of Edelman's selectionist theory of memory in my book *Other Times, Other Realities* (1990). There I understood the familiar repetition compulsion to be a failed attempt to recategorize the affective memory of traumatic experiences. In my book *The Private Self* (1993), I became interested in the problem of the biology of meaning when I recognized that the unconscious mind can be nothing other than a neurophysiological process, but that meaning is in some unknown fashion potentially present as a latent property.

How meaning exists in the unconscious mind as a potential property became clearer to me as a result of the contributions of the linguist George Lakoff and the philosopher Mark Johnson. I owe to them the crucial observation that metaphor is primarily a form of cognition rather than a trope or figure of speech. Further, metaphor as a cognitive tool can operate unconsciously, so that a metaphoric process is one aspect of the unconscious mind. Lakoff and Johnson also emphasized, as I shall do in this book (chapter 4), that metaphor finds its source originally in the body, and that the body, to paraphrase Merleau-Ponty, is an "experiential structure." If we combine Edelman's selectionist principle with Lakoff and Johnson's unconscious metaphoric process, metaphor becomes the selective interpreter of corporeal experience.

Another organizing principle of this book is the assumption that different domains of the mind/brain operate in accordance with different "rules." The algorithmic certainty, point-to-point mappings, and invariance that characterize the "computations" of the visual cortex cannot be applied to the brain's construction of meaning. I join with many other critics who have also observed that algorithms cannot account for thinking in images or fantasy, for error and novelty, or for the fact that the mind can imaginatively bootstrap itself from within. The construction of meaning is not the same as the processing of information; meaning cannot be "represented" by a formal symbolic code. Therefore,

I question the neo-Cartesian concept of representation that has become a basic assumption for many in the cognitive-science community (chapter 1). As a viable alternative to the idea of representation, I turn to Gerald Edelman's and Jean-Pierre Changeux's selectionist theories and the nonlinear dynamics implicit in Walter Freeman's concept of unconscious intentionality.

The construction of meaning requires the use of emotions and feelings as markers of value (chapter 8). Inasmuch as the limbic system, the emotional brain, is of ancient origin, there are homologies between emotions in humans and other species. Therefore, a consideration of evolutionary continuities and discontinuities is an ever-present subtext throughout this book. Unlike other primates, we can delay the expression of emotion, but we, like other primates, are also subject to uncontrollable rages. The amygdala may be the structure that mediates fear in all mammals, including ourselves, but the interpretation of this emotion is another matter. What is singularly human is not only our possession of language but also our capacity for generative imagination, which in turn relies upon the use of metaphor as a cognitive tool. By means of metaphor, feelings can be imaginatively interpreted, displaced, and transformed. Feelings can be "sublimated," which is an exclusively human facility (chapter 7).

The question of evolutionary continuities and discontinuities also appears in the relationship between consciousness, feelings, and the self (chapter 5). I assume, as have others, that mammals are conscious and are conscious of their feelings. Consciousness of feelings may constitute a "protoself" or a "biological self" that functions as a monitor of homeostasis and a consciousness of somatic boundaries so that self and nonself can be distinguished. But very few species other than ourselves have a capacity for recognizing oneself in a mirror. Whether we alone as a species have the capacity for self-reflection, which differs from self-recognition, is a controversial and unsettled issue. I will also examine the question of whether higher primates, such as chimpanzees, possess a theory of mind that can attribute a complex intentionality to others (chapter 9).

In chapter 10, I explore the implications of "mirror neurons" and present several speculative theories regarding the coevolution of metaphor and language. In the closing chapter (chapter 11), I examine the significance of experience in relation to the philosophical mind/body problem. The experience of consciousness should be distinguished from the functions of consciousness. If one accepts this distinction, one must also accept that an epistemic pluralism is needed if we are to achieve a better understanding of the functions of the brain.

Acknowledgments

As this book represents a blend of several disciplines, including some in which I am far from expert, I have needed to rely on the judgments of others to avoid significant errors. It is a pleasure to acknowledge the following friends and colleagues who have read and criticized the manuscript in its entirety or in part. My thanks and gratitude are extended to Gerald Edelman, Walter Freeman, Toni Greatrex, John Kerr, Lewis Kirschner, Jaak Panksepp, David Pincus, Dominique Scarfone, Irving Singer, and my wife Lora Tessman. Any residual misunderstandings are, of course, my own.

Imagination and the
Meaningful Brain

1   Uncertain Steps toward a Biology of Meaning

Metaphor is the great human revolution, at least on a par with the invention of the wheel. . . . Metaphor is a weapon in the hand-to-hand struggle with reality.

Yehuda Amichai

The ultimate goal of neurobiology is to discover how the mind works. When meaning is constructed, a transformation takes place in the brain that is experienced by the mind. A crucial problem for neuroscience is to explain how "matter becomes imagination."[1] The development of a biology of meaning is therefore intrinsically multidisciplined and requires, as I shall try demonstrate throughout this book, an epistemic pluralism.

The investigation of meaning requires an interdisciplinary effort that includes the philosophy of language, linguistics, cognitive science, neurobiology, and psychoanalysis. All of these studies differ in their observational methods, and every specialist, like the proverbial blind men and the elephant, approach the problem from their own perspective. I will claim that the third-person perspective of neuroscience, in its attempt to find the neural correlates of psychological processes, needs also to be augmented by the phenomenology of introspection and the intersubjective knowledge of a two-person relationship. This is especially important with regard to the investigation of imagination, emotion, and feeling. But attempts to explain the meaning of experience has been, for millennia, within the domain of philosophy, and philosophers have shaped the way psychologists have thought about this problem.

Jerome Bruner (1990) describes how in the 1950s he and his colleagues attempted to establish meaning as *the* central concept in psychology. They attempted to restore the concept of meaning to a behavioral psychology and to a psychoanalysis under the sway of a mechanistic instinct theory. Bruner notes that with the advent of the computational theory of mind, information theory has replaced a concept of meaning. Bruner makes the cogent point that the *construction* of meaning is very different from the *processing* of information.

With a few important exceptions, for nearly 2,500 years the problem of meaning, when considered by philosophers, has been separated from the brain, from the body, and from human nature.[2] Traditionally, philosophy has debated the problem of meaning in the context of language: how is it possible that words and sentences "correspond" to things in the physical world? The problem of meaning was seen as a problem of reference: How can something in one domain, that of the mind, refer or "correspond" to something else in another domain, that of the world? How do words and sentences "represent" things in the external world? Within philosophy, an examination of meaning was invariably linked to the question of truth. What guarantees a truthful "correspondence" between words, thoughts, and objects? There is a further problem: How is it conceivable that meaning is at the same time both conventional and private? How can the same word mean the same thing to different people if, as Humpty Dumpty said, "When I use a word, it means just what I choose it to mean neither more nor less."

Turner (1992) has suggested that philosophy ignored the view of the fifth-century Attic philosopher Protagoras, who proposed that man is the measure of all things. Protagoras, as Hilary Putnam notes (1990), was the first deconstuctionist. He appears as an off-stage character in Plato's *Theaetetus* (1928, p. 494). Socrates attacks his idea that man is the measure of all things, as it leads to an unsupportable relativism (1928, p. 494). Socrates says, "The same wind is blowing, and yet one of us may be cold and the other not." Wind cannot be defined by subjective experience. Socrates argued that to believe in the subjectivity of knowledge would introduce a relativism so encompassing that one would not be able to agree on the shared and public meaning of words. Therefore, disagreement and agreement between individuals would not be possible.

The enigma of the meaning of meaning has puzzled philosophers for thousands of years. While it may seem perfectly commonsensical that there is a connection between meaning and mind, that the creation of meaning is a process occurring within one's mind/brain and with other minds, this was not the focus of understanding of traditional philosophy and what has been described as "first generation" cognitive science (Lakoff and Johnson 1999). Traditional philosophy and an earlier generation of cognitive scientists have assumed what has come to be called an "objectivist," or disembodied view—that human nature and the mind/brain play no role in the establishment of meaning. Surprisingly, meaning was believed, until recently, to be generated by a formal symbolic process that was independent of minds and bodies.[3] Can one still believe that meaning is disembodied if one hears Robert Graves define a "true poem" as one in which "the hairs stand on end, the eyes water, the throat is constricted, the skin crawls and a shiver runs down the spine" (1948, p. 24)? Hilary Putnam affirms that meaning is not created through the translation of a cryptographer's code but that meaning is *interactive* and "it depends not just on what is in our heads but also on what is in our environment" (1988). Putnam is essentially describing an ecological theory of mind: meaning is embodied in a mind, which in turn is conjoined to the environment.

A Tendency to Dehumanize the Mind

Today, when the investigation of consciousness and meaning has become a legitimate goal of neuroscience, there has occurred, ironically, within the past decades, a countermovement in psychiatry that has resulted in the dehumanization of the mind. The meaning of human experience is no longer viewed as significant. In 1948, when I started training as a resident in psychiatry, psychiatry's appeal as a profession was that it combined both science and humanism. Fifty years ago, one attempted to understand the patient's narrative and inner life and yet at the same time relate that knowledge to some kind of coherent scientific theory. At the beginning of the twenty-first century, psychiatry in the United States remains in the grip of a pharmacological scientism, a world of neuromodulators. Psychiatry has lost interest in the patient's inner life—the inner meaning of mental disorders is considered to be irrelevant to their treatment and etiology. Consequently, psychiatry has become nearly mindless. Today I feel alienated from psychiatry and hardly recognize it as the same discipline that I once embraced.

This flight away from a meaningful mind is widespread and not confined to psychiatry. This tendency may represent an aspect of American culture that is relatively intolerant of conflict and the disorder that is part of one's inner world, and that welcomes the orderliness of "objective" and presumably scientific explanations of how the mind works. These same cultural forces are one among many elements that contributed to the depreciation of Freud and psychoanalysis in the United States, in contrast to Europe. I agree with Jonathan Lear (1998) that Freud is only a stalking horse, that the culture war is really about the nature of the human soul, the depth and complexity of mind, and the fact that motivation and meaning are derived from the unconscious mind, of which we are only partially aware and which we cannot control.

In a *New Yorker* interview (May 8, 2000) the novelist Philip Roth said, "In the first half of the twentieth century the whole intellectual and artistic effort was to see *behind* things, and that is no longer of interest. To explore consciousness was the great mission of the first half of the century—whether we're talking about Freud or Joyce, whether we're talking about Surrealists or Kafka or Marx or Frazer or Proust or whatever. The whole effort was to expand our sense of what consciousness is and what lies behind it. It's no longer of interest. I think what we're seeing is the narrowing of consciousness. I read the other day in a newspaper that Freud was a kind of charlatan or something worse. This great, tragic poet, our Sophocles!"

Stephen Toulmin (1990), a historian of science and philosophy, believes that the philosopher's "quest for certainty" is a sign of social disorder. He believes that Descartes' attempt to mathematize the human mind, which I shall shortly discuss, was a consequence of the terrible social upheavals that followed from the Thirty Years War, fought between Catholics and Protestants. Descartes' quest for pure reason can be interpreted as a refuge from the destructive effects of passionate controversy. Toulmin reasoned that in times of great social disruption one finds comfort in a philosophy that is formal, timeless, and unchanging. He contrasted Descartes' "quest for certainty" with the intellectual culture of the late Renaissance, exemplified by writers such as Montaigne, who accepted pluralism and uncertainty. If Toulmin's hypothesis is correct, the contemporary effort among some cognitive scientists to find symbolic logic or linear algorithms in the mind/brain may be an unconscious response to the madness that has characterized the terrible twentieth century.

Descartes needed to believe that the mind could in fact be disengaged from emotion, that the mind, when occupied with clear and distinct ideas, existed in an ontologically separate realm from that of the body and its passions. It is seductive and comforting to believe in pure reason uncontaminated by emotion, for it promises the illusion of being in absolute control of the mind and its thoughts. Despite the fact that Freud irreversibly changed this view of human nature, the study of emotion has remained the stepchild of neuroscience. Freud attributed this resistance to accepting the influence of unconscious motivation to seeing it as a threat to man's narcissism—that the ego is not even master in his own house. The discovery of the unconscious, was the third of similar threats to our narcissism and megalomania, the former two being the Copernican and Darwinian revolutions.

This craving for objectivity, according to Putnam (1990), can be found in the belief that perfection can be realized in measurement and what cannot be quantifiable is neither scientific nor objective. Putnam's use of the term *craving* is apt in that the quest for certainty can have the force of an addiction. For decades, under the influence of behaviorism, many psychologists viewed the mind as an unknowable "black box." Today there has been a 180 degree turn, and for some investigators the opposite is true: the mind can be mathematized and known with certainty (Werbos 1993). What may be at issue here is the linear mathematical formalism associated with a computational metaphor. As Arturo Rosenbluth and Norbert Wiener observed, "The price of metaphor is eternal vigilance."[4]

The Australian philosopher Tim van Gelder (1998, p. 427) has provided an elegant argument for substituting a dynamic-systems hypothesis for the prevailing computational analogy. I suspect that neuroscience is at the beginning of a paradigm shift that will gradually recognize a very different model derived from nonlinear dynamics that incorporates indeterminism and uncertainty (for example, see Freeman 1999a, 1999b, and for a discussion of the formalism of nonlinear dynamics, see Kelso 1999).

Some who embrace a computational theory of mind do so with a religious intensity. The philosopher John Searle (1997) noted this when he challenged the belief that a computer's artificial intelligence could serve as an analogy of the mind.[5] Searle (1997) reported that the response to his criticism from adherents to a computational theory of mind has been as passionate and of such religious intensity as if he had attacked the idea of a soul.

It is important to recognize that these contemporary controversies have their eighteenth-century antecedents. This can be illustrated in the views of two philosophers: Descartes and Vico. Descartes' influence on cognitive science has been enormous. The computational view of mind can be traced to Descartes' intent to mathematize the human soul.[6] On the other hand, Vico, whose intuition anticipates many of the ideas that I will present in this book, is known only to the specialist. I would much prefer that their influence were reversed.

With the famous exception of Eccles (1993), there are practically no neurobiologists who believe in a Cartesian dualism—the separation of matter from mind.[7] However, vestiges of Descartes' hope to express mental process in the language of mathematics can be noted by the persistence in the use of the term "compute" as a description of the mind/brain. While the metaphor of the mind/brain as a computer has nearly disappeared, the linear determinism implicit in a "computational" metaphor still persists. For example, Stephen Pinker describes the computational theory of mind as "one of the great ideas in intellectual history" (1997). Although he rejects the analogy of mind as computer, he characterizes psychology as "the analysis of mental software."

It is estimated that the human brain has 100 billion neurons and each neuron may have 10,000 synapses (Changeux and Connes 1995). This literally astronomical potential for synaptic connections in a human brain cannot be duplicated by computers; the scale of a computer-generated model of the brain is similar to that of an insect- or worm-sized brain. But even a worm-sized brain, such as *C. elegans* with its 302 neurons, is extremely complex (Koch and Laurent 1999).

However, I would not at all question the usefulness of computer-generated models of the mind or the use of mathematical models to describe functional brain states, such as suggested by Kelso (1999; see also Tononi and Edelman 1998).

It has been presumed by many in the cognitive-science community that the brain has precise circuits that store signals in a more or less orderly and coded fashion. The assumption is that there is a cerebral code that corresponds to the information received from the external world and from within the brain itself. The accepted view is that coding occurs through variations in synaptic amplitude. The supposition here is that the world is the source of information in the form of coded signals, which is then correspondingly "represented" in the mind. Information theory is incompatible with our uniquely human imaginative capacities, which enable the mind/brain to bootstrap itself from within. The brain could be said to create its own information, but that is not how this metaphor is usually applied. The psychologist Sir Frederick Bartlett, in his classic monograph *Remembering*, made special note "of the organism's capacity to turn around upon its own schemata and construct them afresh" (1932, p. 213). If the mind turns around upon its own schemata, it does not mirror the outside world. Again, we must underline the observation that the *construction* of meaning is very different from the *processing* of information. Walter Freeman's *Societies of Brains* (1995) and his *How Brains Make Up Their Minds* (1999b), Gerald Edelman's trilogy describing his theory of neuronal group selection (1987, 1989, 1992), and Fred Keijzer's *Representation and Behavior* (2001, p. 409) can all be read as a refutation of information theory and coded representations.[8]

Creating artificial neural nets with weighted nodal points, also known as parallel distributed processing, or connectionism, is a closer analogy to neural functioning, as compared to the manipulation of symbols, but at best it is but a very crude analogy. Even animals with very simple nervous systems do not evidence constant weights at synaptic junctions (Koch and Laurent 1999).[9] Conceptual models of the brain/mind are in the nature of thought experiments. Whether such models reflect how the brain actually works remains an open question.

The idea of linear algorithms as a functional unit of the mind/brain has been criticized from many diverse points of view—by neurobiologists such as Gerald Edelman (1992)[10] and Walter Freeman[11] (1995, p. 125; 1999a, 1999b), by the philosopher John Searle (1997), and by the mathematician Roger Penrose (1989), who notes that algorithms do not correspond to how mathematicians think. Some linguists also oppose a computational theory of mind; they include George Lakoff[12] and Gilles Fauconnier (1994). A deep and profound objection to the algorithmic model of the brain can be found in the viewpoint of the Nobel prize-winning chemist Ilya Prigogine (1997), who believes that the universe, which includes our bodies and brains, is not deterministic but probabilistic.

All of these critics have noted that algorithms cannot account for thinking in images, for fantasy and imaginary thoughts, for error, or for novelty. How can the logic of the algorithm be applied to dreams and fantasies? Implicit in the view that the algorithm is the functional unit of the mind/brain is the hope for an eventual reductionism, which philosophers describe as "identity theory," a presumed identity between material events and psychological events. (I will discuss this further in chapter 11.)

Descartes and Vico: Two Antithetical Views of the Mind

As I noted, the hope that mind can be mathematized can be traced to Descartes. This is also true regarding the concept of *representation*, which is central to cognitive science. The Cartesian concept of a representation in the mind that corresponds to objects in the world is also an implicit component of information theory.[13] For this reason, it is worthwhile to review Descartes' ideas in greater detail.

Descartes, who systematized analytic geometry, intended to apply a similar geometric precision to the mind by introducing the doctrine of "clear and distinct ideas," which are potentially quantifiable and organized in accord with a formal logic. If one accepts the fact that the mind contains clear and distinct ideas, those ideas could be subject to the formal logic of geometry (Gaukroger 1995). In Isaiah Berlin's words, "These ultimate *atomic entities of thought* were conceived as being connected with one another by 'necessary' logical links [which can be] mathematically described" (1976). Although Descartes separated mind from the natural world, he believed that the same formal logic by means of which science has obtained control and understanding of the physical world could be applied to the mind, provided one accepts his original premise that thoughts are clear and distinct ideas. To preserve clear and distinct ideas, Descartes needed to separate the corporeal passions from the mind / soul, which is immaterial and without extension. Descartes' idea of atomic entities connected by logical links still pervades the thought of some researchers in contemporary cognitive science, especially those who believe that meaning can be equated to a formal symbolic logic, a "mental code." For example, this aspect of Cartesian thought has reappeared as "mentalese," a term introduced by the philosopher and former colleague of Chomsky, Jerry Fodor (1983). Fodor at one time believed that there is a mental code that corresponds to and mirrors reality.[14] Chomsky's theory of syntax, a theory of formal rules of interpretation, has reinforced this neo-Cartesianism. Implicit in this is a further assumption—that language and thought can be conflated. This view of the mind has been extensively attacked by Hilary Putnam (1988), Gerald Edelman (1992, p. 43), and Lakoff and Johnson (1999).

Until the recent demise of logical positivism, traditional philosophers also believed that meaning could be defined by means of formal logic and therefore objectified. Belief in the objectivity of meaning required that one accept the concepts of *correspondence* and *representation* to account for the constant and truthful relation between what is represented in the mind and what exists in the physical world. Descartes' answer to the question of what guarantees the constancy of a connection between thoughts, words, and things is the existence of a benevolent God who would not play tricks on his subjects. That a *representation* in the mind, such as an idea of an object, matched the object itself assumed God's benevolence. Objective reality was a property of an omnipotent and infinite God. As God is the creator of all things, man's finite, subjective knowledge is a representation of God's view, and therefore a *correspondence* exists between man's subjective, finite knowledge and objective reality. This, Descartes believed, was one proof of God's existence. The flavor of Descartes' conception of *representation* and *correspondence* can be obtained from the following quotation. Descartes stated,

I understand a supreme God, eternal, infinite, omnipotent, the Creator of all things which are outside of Himself, has certainly more objective reality in itself than those by which finite substances are represented.... [To say that] external things exist subjectively and formally in themselves, but objectively or ideally in the understanding, means (as is evident) merely that an idea should agree with the thing of which it is the idea; and that it *hence contains nothing of a representative nature which is not really in the thing itself,* and represents more reality in proportion as the thing it represents contains more reality in itself. (1641, vol. 2, p. 157; my emphasis)

This Cartesian concept of the correspondence of ideas in the mind to objects in the world has been discarded by a contemporary philosophy that no longer believes in a correspondence theory of truth. But the notion of mental representation is still very much with us. The term *representation* is sometimes used in a very broad sense to denote *all mental processes* (the world "represented" in the mind). But when the term is used to refer to a *specific* content that is "represented" in the mind, there may be a naive assumption that the representation (in the mind) correspondingly mirrors what exists in the world. There is, as I have noted earlier, a growing literature within neurobiology and cognitive science that refutes the concept of representation, and I would venture that the lifespan of the concept of representation is limited. The mind/brain does not represent or mirror reality; it *constructs* a virtual reality of its own. Rodolfo Llinás in *I of the Vortex* observes that the brain is a "reality emulator, that we are basically dreaming machines that construct virtual models of the real world" (2001). A representation theory of mind cannot be reconciled to the instability of perceptual illusions or to the fact that the object constructed in the mind does not correspond to the physical object in the world (see, for example, Crick 1994). The concept of representation cannot explain Ramachandran's observations of phantom limbs, where patients construct experiences that do not exist in the physical world (Ramachandran and Blakeslee 1998).[15] In chapter 10, I will discuss the possibility that "mirror neurons" may offer an alternative neural explanation that may eventually substitute for the essentially misleading philosophical concept of representation.

Vico's Poetic Logic and the Embodiment of Mind

The need for an epistemological pluralism that I noted earlier was first advanced by the Italian philosopher Giambattista Vico (1668–1744). He initially recognized the distinction between self-knowledge and knowledge of social institutions of which we are the authors, on the one hand, and knowledge of the natural world that exists outside of our minds and that would remain even if we did not exist, on the other. This is the distinction that Dilthey, a century later, characterized as human studies, (*Geisteswissenschaft*) versus natural science (*Naturwissenschaft*). Empathic knowledge of the self and the other and third-person observations will remain different ways of knowing, but the establishment of a biology of *meaning* will, I hope, include first-, second-, and third-person perspectives.[16] So a biology of meaning may eventually straddle this epistemological divide.

Giambattista Vico was born in 1668, 72 years after Descartes. Although he is today thought to be Italy's most famous philosopher, his influence has been nearly completely overshadowed by Descartes. The reasons for Vico's relative obscurity are many. His style, unlike Descartes', was undisciplined. Further, he was not a clear or coherent thinker. Isaiah Berlin observed, "Vico has not enough talent for his genius." Consequently, his fate has been to be repeatedly forgotten and rediscovered.

What Descartes would completely deny and what Vico was the first to discover is that *meaning is embodied in our total affective interest in the world* (Edie 1969). (*Affective interest* is a concept similar to Freud's concept of cathexis, as I shall describe in chapter 8.) Vico further stated, "*Meaning is constructed through imaginatively entering into the minds of others.*" Vico did not share Descartes' quest for certainty but, in a more pluralistic tradition, accepted what was only probable. Further, Vico proposed what we would now describe as an evolutionary concept of mind. In 1744, when Vico's *New Science* was published, biology was not yet recognized as a separate discipline, and Darwinian evolution was more than a century in the future. Vico proposed that in the course of cultural evolution, the human mind *evolved linguistically*, which resulted in historically different stages of consciousness and different constructions of reality. Vico anticipated a similar hypothesis introduced by the psychologist Merlin Donald (1991) and the archeologist Steven Mithin (1996). It seems to me probable that in human evolution the acquisition of a cognitive capacity for metaphoric thought occurred before the acquisition of language and that the capacity to use conceptual metaphor and the acquisition of language evolved separately. (The evolution of metaphor and language will be discussed in chapter 10.)

Vico wrote that initially humans were without language and communicated by means of signs and gestures. Metaphor was then the primary mode of knowing and understanding the world. With the acquisition of metaphor, the world was interpreted animistically, thunder was a god, and reality was structured in accordance with myth. Vico said, "Every metaphor is a fable in brief" (1744, p. 129). He described *an animistic world in which the structure of mind was projected outwards as a metaphor derived from bodily experience.*

In fact, metaphor was understood not as a figure of speech, a trope, but as a vital means of understanding the world. (This observation waited to be rediscovered by philosophers and linguists such as Lakoff and Johnson [1999] at the end of the twentieth century.) Ralph Waldo Emerson, who was not acquainted with Vico, said, "The world is emblematic. Parts of speech are metaphors, because the whole of nature is a metaphor of the human mind" (1847, p. 18).

Vico further stated, "It is noteworthy that in all languages the greater part of the expressions relating to inanimate things are formed by *metaphors from the human body and its parts and from the human senses and passions*" (1744, p. 405; my emphasis). Vico knew that metaphor is derived from the body and its affective experiences. This is a theme that I shall develop in chapter 4.

Vico opposed the view of the scholastics and Descartes that human nature is lawful, fixed, static, and unchanging. It is important for us to recognize that his work foreshadowed controversies that are still very much alive today. Although neurobiology has unquestionably demonstrated the plasticity of the human brain, there are those who still argue that human nature has been fixed in its genetic adaptation to a late Pleistocene environment and has therefore remained unchanged for 25,000 years (Tooby and Cosmides 1990). Those who believe in an unchanging human nature also argue for a strong genetic determinism of the mind (Dawkins 1976 and Wilson 1998).

I mentioned that it has been Vico's fate to be continually forgotten and rediscovered. For example, John Searle, without citing Vico, stated in his monograph *The Mystery of Consciousness* (1997), "The really important distinction is not between the mental and the physical, mind and body, but between those real features of the world that exist independently of observers—such as force, mass and gravitational attraction—and those features that are dependent upon observers—such as money, property, marriage and government." (This is the heart of Vico's argument.) All these cultural institutions—such as money, property, marriage, and government—exist only because of the meaning that we attribute to them. Vico would describe such institutions as man's construction. As such, they can be better known, as products of our mind, than nonhuman nature, which we can only observe from the outside. We no longer believe, as Vico did, that introspective and empathic knowledge is superior to scientific knowledge. Today most cognitive scientists and neurobiologists dismiss such knowledge as merely anecdotal, and yet every scientist who investigates consciousness makes use of their own introspection. I will reiterate: *when investigating a biology of meaning, we need to accept a pluralistic epistemology that combines a first- and second-person (intersubjective) perspective with the traditional third-person perspective of neuroscience.* The need for this epistemic pluralism was also recognized by the philosopher of science Herbert Feigl (1958) and neuroscientists Francisco Varela (1999) and Max Velmans (2000).

In his essay on the mind/brain problem (1958), Feigl argues for a "double" knowledge, referring both to phenomenology and introspection and to neurophysiology. This topic as it relates to the mind-body problem will be discussed further in chapter 11.

Intentionality as a Biological Concept

Meaning is sometimes equated with *intentionality*. The philosophical concept of intentionality is attributed to Franz Brentano (1838–1927), whose lectures Freud attended when he was a medical student in 1874. Whether Freud was influenced by Brentano is not at all clear (Jones 1953). Intentionality refers to directing the mind toward an object. Brentano believed that what defines mental states is their intentionality, that is to say, that mental states invariably are *about something*. Brentano also included within the concept of intentionality, the mental "inexistence" of an object, so intentionality includes the imagination. This conception invites the recognition that intentionality must also encompass the unconscious mind's relation to the world. However, the term *intentionality* usually refers, in philosophical discourse, to the conscious mind's relation to the world. It is in this sense that, following Brentano, the philosopher John Searle (1983) defines intentionality as "directedness or aboutness," a "mind-to-world direction of fit." Searle concludes, as I do, that "intentional states are realized in the neurophysiology of the brain."

A first step toward a biology of meaning requires a broadening of the concept of intentionality. If intentionality is to be brought into a biological context, the direction of fit between brain/minds and the world cannot remain at the descriptive level of "aboutness." Aboutness is unidirectional. If the philosopher's definition of intentionality is to be converted into a biological intentionality, we must posit a more complex relationship between the mind/brain and its environment. Such a relationship between the organism in the environment was described by the geneticist Richard Lewontin. He said, "The external forces, what we usually think of as 'environment,' are themselves partly a consequence of the activities of the organism itself as it produces and consumes the conditions of its own existence. Organisms do not find the world in which they develop. They make it" (1991, p. 105). The neurobiologist Walter Freeman

(1995, 1999b) proposed a more truly biological concept of intentionality as an interactive, ecological concept. Freeman proposed that "meanings arise as a brain creates intentional behaviors and *then changes itself* in accordance with the sensory consequences of those behaviors." To avoid the errors implicit in Descartes' concept of mental representation, Freeman embraced the idea of intentionality as described by Thomas Aquinas in 1272. Thomas Aquinas defined intentionality as the process by which humans and other animals act in accordance with their own growth and maturation. *An "intent" is the directing of action toward some future goal that is defined and chosen by the actor.* Intentionality, as redefined in this pre-Cartesian manner, is quite different from the term as used by Brentano and other philosophers such as Searle (1983). Intentionality as redefined here is not about "aboutness." Meaning is achieved through *action* in the world, and in turn, the self is altered by that action. Freeman's redefinition of intentionality, therefore, also includes the idea of assimilation—the self changes itself as a result of what it has encountered as a consequence of its actions. Aquinas' definition of intentionality includes the imagination, as intentionality refers to actions at a future time. Although Thomas Aquinas describes intentionality as directing action toward some future goal defined and chosen by the actor, it should also be understood that intentionality is fundamentally an *unconscious* process, that the self is not necessarily a conscious agent. (I will discuss the self and intentionality in greater detail in chapter 5.) Intentionality so redefined also includes the idea of mental construction by means of selection that is based on forming hypotheses and testing the environment, in contrast to a mental construction that is based on the representation of information. This is a point of view that is consistent with the pragmatic philosophy of William James and John Dewey, as well as the ecological approach to perception proposed by Piaget (1954), James Gibson (1986), and Andy Clark (1997). "Intentionality differs from a 'motive,' which is the reason and explanation of the action, and from a 'desire,' which is the awareness and experience stemming from the intent" (Freeman 1999b). This definition is fully in accord with Vico's understanding that "meaning is embodied in our total affective interest in the world."

The philosopher Merleau-Ponty's formulation of "the intentional arc" (1962), which "projects around about us our past, our future, our human setting," resulting in "maximum grip," is also fully consistent with Aquinas' concept of intentionality. Freeman believes that the intentional arc names *the tight connection between the agent and the world,* that as the agent acquires skills, those skills are "stored," not as representations in the mind, but as *dispositions* to respond to the solicitations of situations in the world. Freeman not only affirms the existence of a biology of meaning but also recognizes that mappings between the mind and the world are intersubjective. Further, Freeman observed in his research on the reaction of rabbits' brains to odors (which will be described in chapter 5) that there was no invariance between the environmental stimuli and the response in the rabbit's brain. The rabbit's brain does not respond to a symbolically coded message; instead, the *individual rabbit uniquely determined the "meaning" of the stimuli.* Freeman concluded that "the bulbar patterns [in the rabbits' brains] were signs of the meaning of the stimuli for the subjects, not of the stimuli as we observers knew them" (1993). Not only was there a failure to observe invariance between the stimulus and the individual rabbit's response, but the response of each individual rabbit was different from the others.

The Mind Turning Around on Itself

The transformation of the philosopher's concept of intentionality into a biological concept is a first step toward a biological theory of meaning. The goal-directed mind/brain takes *action* in the environment and thereby changes itself. For humans, however, and perhaps for some other primates as well, meaning is created not only in interaction with the environment. In humans the imagination can bootstrap intentionality in the absence of immediate sensory inputs. Llinás describes the brain as "primarily a self-activating system whose organization is geared toward the generation of intrinsic images" (2001). Llinás believes that the consciousness of the dream state, when we are cut off from sensory inputs, is a closer analogy to waking consciousness. He emphasizes, as I shall do, that although the mind is activated by sensory inputs, it is also a self-contained system. Freud suggested something similar. He proposed that the unconscious mind/brain is "perceived" as an internal environment, which can become a substitute for the external environment, a second universe. Meaning may be constructed entirely from within. In a profound and somewhat ambiguous passage, Freud wrote the following: "In psychoanalysis there is no choice for us but to assert that mental processes are themselves unconscious and to liken the perception of them by means of consciousness to the perception of the external world by means of the sense-organs" (1915b, p. 171). The psychologist Nicholas Humphrey (1997) interpreted this and the following Freudian citation as evidence that Freud believed that consciousness functioned as an "inner eye," a kind of metasense organ that covered the entire mind.

Fifteen years earlier in *The Interpretation of Dreams* (1900), Freud wrote the following: "The psychical apparatus, which is turned towards the external world with its sense organs of the perceptual system, is itself the external world in relation to the sense organs of consciousness." Freud is proposing two interconnected ideas that are entirely consistent with contemporary neurobiology: one is the self-evident idea that consciousness receives impressions from both the external world and the body's interior, but what Freud adds is not self evident—that sensations are received from the unconscious inner world and are elaborated as feelings in a way that is *analogous* to how sensations are received from the external world. By stating that the psychical apparatus is itself the external world in relation to the sense organs of consciousness, Freud intuited that consciousness not only responded to internal somatic sensations, but that its internal monitoring is analogous to perceiving the external world. He was describing both the bodily sources of the experience of the self and more important, *that the inner world of the self is an alternative universe.* One might say that the inner world of the self is a *virtual* universe.

Freud's thinking was influenced, as he acknowledged (1915b, p. 171), by Kant, who taught that our knowledge of the external world is constrained by the structures of the human mind. That the external world "as it is" is essentially unknowable is a realization that has been ever increasingly confirmed by contemporary neurobiology (Solms 1997b). Although we cannot ever know the unconscious "as it is," Freud viewed the unconscious as a *potential* source of meaning. This is a quotation from his paper "The unconscious" (Freud 1915b, p. 167):

We can go further and argue, in support of there being an unconscious psychical state, that at any given moment consciousness includes only a small content, so that the greater part of what we call conscious knowledge must in any case be for a considerable period of time *in a state of latency* [my emphasis], that is to say, of being psychically unconscious. When all our latent memories are taken into consideration, it becomes totally incomprehensible how the existence of the unconscious can be denied. But here we encounter the objection that these latent recollections can no longer be described a psychical, *but they correspond to residues of somatic processes from which what is psychical can once more arise.*

Freud does not say anything further about those "residues of somatic processes"[17] from which what is psychical emerges, but on my reading of this passage, Freud suggests that there is an unknown neurophysiological process from which meaning is generated. Meaning exists as a *potentiality* in the unconscious. In the next chapter I will present a hypothesis that describes the generation of meaning from an unconscious metaphoric process.

2   Metaphor, Memory, and Unconscious Imagination

The imagination is one of the highest prerogatives of man. By this faculty he unites former images and ideas, independently of the will, and thus creates brilliant and novel results. . . . The dream is an involuntary [kind][1] of poetry.

Charles Darwin

Cognitive linguists Lakoff and Johnson (1999) affirm what has long been known: *the source of the imagination, what makes us uniquely human, is an unconscious metaphoric process.* Unconscious autobiographical memory, the memory of the self and its intentions, is constantly recontextualized, and the link between conscious experience and unconscious memory is provided by metaphor. This suggests that the metaphoric process that we recognize in our dreams is also continuously operative while we are awake.

Metaphor as the Currency of Mind

The philosopher Mark Johnson and the linguist George Lakoff (Lakoff and Johnson 1980, Johnson 1987, Lakoff 1987, Lakoff and Johnson 1999) have shown that metaphor is not simply a figure of speech but is primarily a form of thought, a form of cognition. As metaphor is a mode of cognition, metaphor can function as an interpreter of unconscious memory. Our emotional and imaginative life is literally unthinkable apart from this unconscious metaphoric process. As the late novelist and philosopher Iris Murdoch observed, "The development of consciousness in human beings is inseparably connected with the use of metaphor. Metaphors are not merely peripheral decorations or even useful models, they are *fundamental forms of our condition*" (1970; my emphasis). Murdoch's reference to "peripheral decorations" is a specific allusion to Aristotle's concept of metaphors as merely peripheral decorations of language. For centuries, philosophers and linguists, following Aristotle, understood metaphor to be merely a figure of speech, a departure from literal meaning. Aristotle's theory of metaphor has had a remarkable longevity, as philosophers of language and linguists have until recently unquestioningly accepted his definition of metaphor. Aristotle described metaphor as an analogy whose use is a mark of excellence. Aristotle wrote,

A metaphorical word is a word transferred from the proper sense; either from genus to species, or from species to genus, or in the way of an analogy. (1934, p. 40)

The greatest excellence [in the use of words] is to be happy in the use of metaphor; for it is this alone which cannot be acquired, and which, consisting in a quick discernment of resemblances, is a certain mark of genius. (1934, p. 45)

Cognitive linguistics has demonstrated that Aristotle was mistaken in thinking that metaphor is merely a part of speech. Metaphor is a fundamental and uniquely human cognitive ability, a primary form of cognition and thought that becomes secondarily incorporated into language (Johnson 1987, Lakoff 1987, Turner 1991, Gibbs 1994, Lakoff and Johnson 1999). That metaphor exists apart from language is evident in gestures, visual images, feelings, and bodily sensations, which can all function as metaphors. Merlin Donald (1991) has speculated that in the evolution of our species, metaphoric gesture may have preceded the appearance of language. (A discussion of this hypothesis regarding the separate evolution of metaphor appears in chapter 10.) The acquisition of metaphor has probably had a separate evolutionary history; language and metaphor may represent coevolutionary processes.

I define *metaphor,* as does cognitive linguistics, as *a mapping or transfer of meaning between dissimilar domains (from a source domain to a target domain).* Metaphor not only *transfers* meaning between different domains, but by means of novel recombinations metaphor can *transform* meaning and generate new perceptions. Imagination could not exist without this recombinatory metaphoric process.

As a mode of cognition, metaphor is doubly embodied, first, as an unconscious neural process and, second, in that metaphors are generated from bodily feelings, so that it is possible to speak of a corporeal imagination.

The Scientific Imagination as an Unconscious Metaphoric Process

Since the nineteenth century it has been known from the following often quoted account given by the chemist Friederich August von Kekulé that the creative imagination of scientists can be both involuntary and unconscious. Kekulé described how his discovery of the closed-carbon-ring structure of organic compounds occurred unconsciously in a dream. He related that one afternoon in 1865 he fell asleep:

I turned my chair to the fire and dozed, he relates: Again the atoms were gambolling before my eyes. This time the smaller groups kept modestly in the background. My mental eye, rendered more acute by repeated visions of this kind, could now distinguish larger structures, of manifold confirmation; long rows, sometimes more closely fitted together; all twining and twisting in snakelike motion. But look! What is that? One of the snakes had seized hold of its own tail and the form whirled mockingly before my eyes. As if by a flash of lightning I awoke. . . . Let us learn to dream, gentlemen. (Koestler 1964)

That an analogous unconscious process occurs while one is awake is illustrated by an equally famous account of the creativity of the unconscious. Below is an account of the French mathematician Henri Poincaré's discovery or invention of what is called *Fuchsian* functions. Poincaré was convinced that his mathematical creativity was a product of the unconscious mind. He wrote, "Most striking at first is this appearance of sudden illumination, a manifest sign of long, unconscious prior work. The role of this unconscious work in mathematical invention appears to me incontestable." Poincaré provided the following reminiscence:

Just at this time, I left Caen, where I was living, to go on a geological excursion under the auspices of the School of Mines. *The incidents of the travel made me forget my mathematical work.* Having reached Coutances, we entered an omnibus to go someplace or other. At the moment when I put my foot on the step, the idea came to me, without anything in my former thoughts seeming to have paved the way for it, that the transformations I had used to the find the Fuchsian functions were identical with those of non-Euclidian geometry. I did not verify the idea; I should not have had time, as, taking my seat in the omnibus, I went on with the conversation already commenced, but I felt a perfect certainty. On the return to Caen, for conscience's sake, I verified the result at my leisure. (From Hadamard 1945; my emphasis)

Poincaré's unconscious process was primed by his intentionality, his intense desire to discover a solution, but it was then necessary for him divert his attention from this task; as he notes, "The incidents of the travel made me forget my mathematical work."

That the metaphoric process functions apart from language is beautifully illustrated in the following account provided by Einstein in response to an inquiry from the French mathematician Jacques Hadamard, who was investigating the role of the unconscious in mathematical thought.

The words or the language, as they are written or spoken, do not seem to play any role in my mechanism of thought. The psychical entities which seem to serve as elements in thought are certain signs and more or less clear images which can be "voluntarily" reproduced and combined.

There is, of course, a certain connection between those elements and relevant logical concepts. It is also clear that the desire to arrive finally at logically connected concepts is the emotional basis of this rather vague play with the above-mentioned elements. But taken from a psychological viewpoint, this *combinatory play* seems to be the essential feature in productive thought—before there is any connection with logical construction and words or other kinds of signs which can be communicated to others.

The above-mentioned elements are, in any case, *some of visual and some of muscular type.* Conventional words or other signs have to be sought laboriously only in a secondary stage, when the mentioned associative play is sufficiently established and can be reproduced at will.

According to what has been said, the play with the mentioned elements is aimed to be analogous to certain logical connections one is searching for. In a stage when words intervene at all, they

are, in any case, purely auditive but they interfere only in the secondary stage as already mentioned. It seems to me that what you
call full consciousness is a limit case which can never be fully accomplished. This seems to me connected with the fact called the
narrowness of consciousness. (Hadamard 1945; my emphasis)

This excerpt from Einstein's letter to Hadamard does not
refer directly to an unconscious process; rather, he refers to
the "narrowness" of consciousness. He described the "play"
of visual images and, more remarkably, the play of muscular (kinesthetic) sensations, which we can infer are the products of an unconscious metaphoric process. Only later and
secondarily does Einstein revert to language in consideration of the need for communication to others.

The metaphoric process, when operating apart from language, can process fragmentary visual, auditory, and other
bodily sensations. The metaphoric transfer of meaning
can also occur between different sensory modalities, no
matter how fragmented the elements are, such as isolated
sounds of speech. I am reminded of a game described
by the art historian Ernst Gombrich (1960). He invited the
reader to play a game in which language consisted only of
two words: *ping* and *pong*. If we had to name an elephant
and a cat, the answer is evident, for *pong* is "heavier" and
therefore means elephant. So that when Einstein reports
that he *plays with* visual, auditory, and muscular elements, I have no doubt that he is describing a metaphoric
process.

The French mathematician Alain Connes described an unconscious process that generates mathematical thought.[2]
Connes affirms the unconscious nature of mathematical
thought in a published dialogue with the neurobiologist
Jean-Pierre Changeux (Changeux and Connes 1995). Connes
also observed, as did others, the need to suspend conscious

intention for an unconscious process to take place. Connes summarizes his observations:

• There must be a conscious intention of what one wishes to achieve.

• Then this intention must be placed aside.

• One must allow for a period of germination or incubation.

• The unexpected solution appears at times accompanied by great ecstatic joy.

• This is followed by a period of critical evaluation.

Connes reports: "I've often observed too that once the first hurdle of preparation has been gotten over, one runs up against a wall. The main error to be avoided is trying to attack the problem head-on. During the incubation phase, you have to proceed indirectly, obliquely. If you think too directly about a problem, you fairly quickly exhaust the usefulness of the tools accumulated in the course of the first phase, and are apt to become discouraged. Thought needs to be liberated in such a way that subconscious work can take place." Changeux responds: "Is it a matter simply of giving working memory enough to do and giving greater rein to an unconscious process that relies more on long-term memory? Or is it, to the contrary, a kind of associational procedure that takes time because the elements that need to be put together belong to rather different contexts?"

I would reply to Changeux's question by suggesting that the unconscious creative imagination utilizes both (unconscious) long-term memory and an associative process linked by means of metaphor. This is what consumes time during the incubation period. Working memory merely initiates the process of conscious (and unconscious) intention as the day residue incubates a dream.

Does an Unconscious Metaphoric Process Have Neural Correlates?

Let us assume that there is an unconscious metaphoric cognitive process operative in the waking state. What then
might be the neural correlates of such a process? The
hypotheses that I shall describe are only reasonable sur-
mises that reflect an investigator's imagination, but for this
reason alone they should not be depreciated. D. O. Hebb has
commented, "When used by theorists outside of neurology,
'CNS' should be understood to stand not for 'central nervous system,' but for 'conceptual nervous system'" (cited
in Kitcher 1992).

Metaphor formation is intrinsically multimodal, as it
must engage visual, auditory, and kinesthetic inputs. In addition, metaphor formation must access unconscious memory. It is a reasonable assumption, inasmuch as the capacity
for metaphoric thought is uniquely human, that the prefrontal association cortex, which is significantly enlarged in humans as compared to primates, is active in unconscious
metaphor formation (Deacon 1997). It is also known that this
area of the brain has rich connections with the limbic system. Some investigators (Bottini, Corcoran, et al. 1994) suggest that the metaphoric process is predominately within
the right hemisphere, but as metaphor utilizes global
multimodal inputs, I would remain skeptical of such claims.

It is not too difficult to specify what is *not* likely to be
the neural correlates of the metaphoric process. The neural
correlates of the metaphoric process are not at all likely to be
represented by point-to-point invariant maps, such as have
been described for visual perception. As we know more
about visual perception than any other cortical function, this
specialized area of neurophysiology has become a paradigm

from which theories regarding other higher functions of the human mind, such as consciousness and meaning construction, are extrapolated (see, for example, Crick 1994, Pinker 1997). Investigation of the neurophysiology of vision has shown a fixed topographic relation between the receptor cells and the target areas of the cerebral cortex. Further, patterns of neural activity in the retina correspond faithfully to the spatial and temporal details of visual inputs (Tononi and Edelman 1998). In contrast, the neural correlates of metaphoric imagination must be nonlinear and indeterminate. It seems likely that *different domains of the mind operate in accordance with different rules.*

I believe that the selectionist theories of Gerald Edelman (1987, 1989, 1992) and Jean-Pierre Changeux (1997) and the neural dynamics described by Freeman (1999b) offer a more promising paradigm. Edelman proposes a process called *global mapping.* Unlike the relative point-to-point fixation of maps from the retina to the visual cortex or from the musculature to the motor cortex, Edelman believes that maps of higher mental functions are indeterminate. In accordance with his theory of neuronal group selection, neuronal maps do not depend on preexisting codes. This indeterminacy results from what is called a selectionist principle. Edelman proposed that a *somatic selection* analogous to Darwinian natural selection occurs at the level of synapses and neuronal cells within the brain. The selection process takes place in somatic time and is driven by experience and the extensive variability of neural circuitry and neuronal cells (see Edelman 1992 and, for an overview, Edelman 1998).[3]

What is uniquely human is a generative imagination from which the individual can create an internal unseen world. If the neural correlates of a metaphoric process are established, it is likely to reflect some form of bootstrapping, some form of the brain's "turning around upon its own schemata," something analogous to what has been described by Edelman as a "higher order" consciousness that incorporates a capacity for self-reflection. Edelman proposed that a "higher order" consciousness is multilayered and complex, as compared to a comparatively less complex *primary consciousness,* which is "the remembered present" (1992, p. 109). Edelman does not directly propose a neural theory of metaphor or of imagination, but he does suggest that higher mental functions such as the formation of conceptual categories may reflect "higher-order maps," that to construct conceptual categories the brain constructs maps of its own activities, that the brain makes maps of its own maps, which are not fixed topographically. Indeterminism is a necessary attribute of such higher-order functions.

It is likely that the neural correlates of an unconscious metaphoric process would be unpredictable and indeterminate. J. A. Scott Kelso (1999) describes this "functional instability" as a notable characteristic of the brain. The neural correlates of a metaphoric process are likely to be nonlinear.[4]

The French neuroscientist Jean-Pierre Changeux (1997, p. 169) described a plausible hypothesis regarding the neural properties of the "substrate" of imaginative thought. Changeux, who with Edelman is also committed to a neuronal selectionist theory, emphasized the indeterminate nature of what he described as spontaneous recombinations between neural assemblies (maps).

The neurons participating in such assemblies will be both dispersed and multimodal, or perhaps amodal. This should bestow on them very rich "associative" properties, allowing them to link together and above all to combine. Thus, it becomes plausible that such assemblies, made up of oscillatory neurons with high *sponta-neous* activity, could recombine among themselves. *This recombin-*

ing activity would represent a "generator of hypotheses," a mechanism of diversification essential for the genesis of prerepresentations and subsequent selection of new concepts. In a word, it would be the substrate of imagination [my emphasis]. It would also account for the "simulation" of future behavior in the face of a new situation. For a system to organize itself, it is obvious that there must be more than simple creation of diversity. A *selection* is possible, as we have seen, by a comparison of mental objects in terms of their resonance or dissonance. (Changeux 1997, p. 169)

In *Conversations on Mind, Matter, and Mathematics* (Changeux and Connes 1995), Changeux identifies the prefrontal cortex as the area in which such associations are likely to take place. *Let us hypothesize that such associations are formed unconsciously by means of the metaphoric process that combines previously unconnected experiences.* Arthur Koestler expressed a similar idea, referring to metaphor as a bisociative act: "The bisociative act connects previously unconnected matrices of experience; it makes us understand what it is to be awake, to be living on several planes at once" (1964, p. 48). Koestler's idea that metaphor allows one to live "on several planes at once" is precisely what I wish to convey.

Metaphor and the Recontextualization of Memory

The hypothesis of an unconscious metaphoric process must be linked to memory. I believe that our unconscious autobiographical memory, in which emotion is salient, forms potential categories by means of metaphor. To convince you of the reasonableness of this hypothesis, I will describe two theories of memory: one proposed by Freud and the other by Edelman. If memory is organized in accordance with an unconscious metaphoric process, we must assume that autobiographical memory, memory of the self and its intentions, is extremely plastic and subject to constant recontextualization.

I noted in *Other Times, Other Realities* (Modell 1990) the similarities between Freud's theory of memory and Edelman's. Freud and Edelman described memory as a recontextualization. Freud referred to the retranscription of memory as *Nachträglichkeit*, which can be literally translated as a retrospective attribution.[5] Freud's theory of memory as a recontextualization first appeared in a letter from Freud to Fliess dated December 6, 1896 (Masson 1985):

> As you know, I am working on the assumption that our psychic mechanism has come into being by process of stratification: the material present in the form of memory traces being subjected from time to time to *a rearrangement* in accordance with fresh circumstances—to a *retranscription*. Thus what is essentially new about my theory is the thesis that memory is present not once but several times over, that it is laid down in various kinds of indications. . . . I should like to emphasize the fact that the successive registrations represent the psychic achievement of successive epochs of life. At the boundary between such two such epochs a translation of the psychic material must take place. I explain the peculiarities of the psychoneurosis by supposing that this translation has not taken place in the case of some of the material, which has certain consequences.

One basic function of memory is the detection of novelty, the detection of similarity and differences within the ever-changing flood of perceptions from inside the body and from the outer world. The sorting of similarity and difference is another way of describing category formation. Categorization is a function of memory, and memory, in turn, is a property of neural systems. Memory, an ancient property of biological systems, can be broadly defined as the ability to repeat a performance under changing contexts. I quote now from Edelman 1998:

Memory has properties that allow perception to alter recall, and recall to alter perception. It has no fixed capacity limit, since it actually generates "information" by construction. It is possible to envision how it could generate semantic capabilities prior to syntactical ones. If such a view is correct, *every active perception is to some degree an act of creation, and every act of memory is to some degree an act of imagination.* (My emphasis)

Edelman viewed memory as invariably linked to category formation. He said, "Until a particular individual in a particular species categorizes it in an adaptive fashion, the world is an unlabeled place in which novelty is frequently encountered" (Edelman 1989, p. 4). Therefore, the primordial task faced by the brain is that of labeling an unlabeled world. This is accomplished by means of perceptual and conceptual categories. "A memory is the enhanced *ability* to categorize associatively, not the storage of features of attributes as lists" (Edelman 1987, p. 241). In this sense, memory is not representational (this point is enlarged on in Edelman 1998). Memory is not a store of fixed or coded attributes. Instead, memory consists of a process of continual recategorization, which must involve continued motor activity and repeated rehearsal (Edelman 1989, p. 56).

As I noted, some cognitive scientists assume that memory is representational, that memory consists of a codelike record that once corresponded to experience. If memory is representational, the activation of a memory would consist of a static process analogous to retrieving items from a storage bank. Edelman's theory of recategorization evokes a very different concept. Memory retrieval is selective, depending on the context of the immediate experience. Memory does not capture a coded representation but is itself a construction. Unconscious memory exists only as a latent *potential* awaiting reconstruction.

Psychic Trauma and the Impaired Recontextualization of Memory

Clinical observation leads to the unmistakable conclusion that psychological trauma may result in a failure to recategorize or recontextualize memory. The inability to recontextualize memory determines whether a given experience will prove to be traumatic. As we have different methods at our disposal with which to recategorize memory, individuals will react to trauma in their own particular way, so the effect of a given environmental trauma is variable and unpredictable. When there is an inability to recontextualize memory, the experience of the present, the here and now, will be pervaded by memories of the past. In this fashion, trauma will constrict the complexity of consciousness.

The process of the retrieval of traumatic memories gives further support to the hypothesis that an unconscious metaphoric process is operative in the waking state. As the critic and novelist Cynthia Ozick writes, "Metaphor [like the Delphic oracle] is also a priest of interpretation, but what it interprets is memory" (1991). When metaphor is the interpreter of traumatic memories, it interprets with the aid of metonymy (a part substituting for the whole), and metaphoric memorial categories are evoked by metonymic associations. But trauma can be self-sustaining, as trauma will degrade the metaphoric process: here the metaphoric process transfers meaning from the past to the present *without transformation,* and as a consequence imagination is constricted. The past becomes a template for the present, creating a loss of ambiguity in the experience of the here and now; there is an absence of the customary play of similarity and difference. In experiential terms, this means that the present is conflated with the past.

In an example I used in my book *Other Times, Other Realities* (1990), a patient reported the following incident: Because his airline went out on strike, my patient was stranded in a distant city and unable to return home. He did everything possible to obtain passage on another airline: he cajoled and pleaded with the functionaries of other airlines, all to no avail. Although my patient was usually not unduly anxious and was in fact a highly experienced traveler who in the past remained calm under circumstances that would frighten many people, in this particular situation he experienced an overwhelming and generalized panic. He felt as if the unyielding airline representatives were like Nazis and that the underground passages of the airline terminal resembled a concentration camp. The helplessness of not being able to return home, combined with the institutional intransigence of the authorities, evoked the following memory, which had been unconscious.

When this man was three years old, he and his parents were residents of a central European country and, as Jews, were desperately attempting to escape from the Nazis. They did in fact manage to obtain an airline passage to freedom, but until that point, the outcome was very much in doubt. Although my patient did not recall his affective state at that time, his parents reported that he seemed cheerful and unaffected by their anxiety. In this example, his helpless inability to leave a foreign city, combined with the intransigence of the authorities, evoked a specific affect category that remained as a potential memory of an unassimilated past experience. In this example, an unconscious memory was metaphorically interpreted with the help of a metonymic association. His helpless inability to leave a foreign city combined with the intransigence of the authorities served as a metonymic trigger. It would appear that the affective gestalt consisting of his helpless inability to leave plus the intransigence of the authorities was a metaphoric categorical equivalent of the earlier trauma. This metaphorical correspondence triggered a global response in which the differences between the domains of past and present were obliterated and, accordingly, he became intensely frightened. In this example, I believe that an unconscious metaphoric process interpreted a salient emotional unconscious memory, which was then transferred onto present experience. *The traumatic memory of his childhood remained intact, as it had not been recontextualized as a result of later experience.*

Here is a further example. A patient reported that when he was about two or three years old, his mother had a spontaneous miscarriage. He was able to reconstruct that in all probability his mother became "hysterical" and was emotionally distraught for an undetermined period of time. As a witness to these events, he felt as if his mother had gone crazy. As an adult, he was very tolerant of craziness in women if he was not emotionally attached to them, but any sign of irrational thinking on the part of a woman upon whom he was dependent, such as his wife, made him extremely anxious. The metaphoric process created an unconscious affect category—that of irrationality in women upon whom he was dependent. This affective memory was activated and recreated in real time by means of a metonymic association. When he was responding to his wife's "irrational" behavior, the distinction between past and present was obliterated, as in the previous example. The past invaded the present.

If we return to the definition of metaphor as the transfer of meaning between dissimilar domains, the domains here are that of past and present time. An unconscious metaphoric process resulted in the transfer of meaning between the here and now and the memorialized past. Unlike the examples of mathematical imagination that I presented earlier in this chapter, where metaphor led to new combinations of thought, in these cases of trauma, the metaphoric process resulted in the transfer of meaning from the past to the present, but without such transformations. *It can be said that the metaphoric process was foreclosed or frozen.*

The body image suffers a similar fate when there is an absence of perceptual inputs, leading to a failure of recontextualization. This is evident in phantom-limb phenomenon, where there is a failure to update the image of the body due to the absence of sensory inputs from the missing limb (Ramachandran and Blakeslee 1998). The neurologist Ramachandran devised an ingenious method for treating phantom limbs. He restored the absent sensory inputs through an arrangement of mirrors in which an image of the patient's intact limb was substituted for the one that was lost. In some cases the illusion of the phantom limb disappeared because of a recontextualization of the body image.

In *Other Times, Other Realities* (Modell 1990), I referred to the concept of *affect categories.* I was attempting to find a new way of understanding the old psychoanalytic notion of "complexes." A "complex" can be defined as an organized group of ideas and memories of great affective force that are either partly or totally unconscious. I believe that metaphor organizes emotional memory. Inasmuch as category formation is an aspect of memory, metaphor provides the link between emotional memory and current perceptions. I have suggested that a similarity based on a metaphoric

correspondence is the means through which emotional categories are formed. Unconscious emotional memories exist
as *potential* categories, which, in the process of retrieval, are
associatively linked to events in the here and now by means
of metaphor and metonymy. As consciousness is at all times
primarily a *selecting agency* (James 1890), metaphor and metonymy play a salient role.

The Varieties of Conscious and Unconscious Memory Systems

Although there may be innumerable different memory systems in the brain, many cognitive scientists have followed
the lead of the psychologist Endel Tulving (1972), who differentiated experiential memory, which he called *episodic,*
from what he termed *semantic* memory. *Episodic memory is
temporally dated, whereas semantic memory is not.* Semantic
memory refers to knowledge-based memory, the memory
of acquired information not in any sense autobiographical.

Another well-known category of memory is that of *procedural* memory, the memory of motor routines, such as learning to ride a bicycle or learning to play the piano. Unlike
episodic memory, which can potentially become conscious,
implicit procedural memory is incapable of becoming conscious. That is to say, we cannot consciously recall (without
performing the action) the sequence of motor acts required
to ride a bicycle or tie our shoelaces. Procedural memory is
without meaning and has no relation to metaphor.

Some cognitive scientists and neurobiologists mistakenly
believe that implicit or procedural memory is the only form
of unconscious memory, I would judge this opinion to be a
profound misunderstanding. This is a significant point of
disagreement between psychoanalysis and neuroscience re-

garding the nature of the unconscious. Psychoanalysts believe unquestionably that the unconscious is a source of potential meaning—that the unconscious does not consist only of the memory of motor routines. What Tulving calls *episodic* (autobiographical) memory is also unconscious, especially the memory of unassimilated experiences. Unlike procedural memory, episodic memory, the memory of the history of the self, is always potentially meaningful.

To limit the unconscious to the memory of motor routines is totally at odds with the hypothesis of an unconscious metaphoric process that assumes unconscious memory to be *potentially* meaningful. As we shall see, this is a very important issue, for it is based on certain philosophical assumptions concerning the definition of mind. (I discuss this issue further in chapter 11.) There are many in the cognitive-science community who would limit the definition of mind to conscious experience and who believe that only procedural memory is implicit or unconscious. As procedural memory is devoid of semantic content, this view of human psychology is reminiscent of a discredited behaviorism that achieved a certain clarity by eliminating the mind.

What follows is Tulving's description of the distinction between episodic and semantic memory:

Episodic memory receives and stores information about temporally dated episodes or events, and temporal-spatial relations among these events. A perceptual event can be stored in the episodic system solely in terms of its perceptible properties or attributes, and it is always stored in terms of its autobiographical references to the already existing contents of the episodic memory store.

Semantic memory is the memory necessary for the use of language. It is a mental thesaurus of organized knowledge a person possesses about words and other verbal symbols, their meaning and referents, about relations among them, and about roles,

formulas and algorithms for the manipulation of the symbols, concepts and relations. Semantic memory does not register perceptual
properties of inputs, but rather cognitive referents to input signals.
The semantic system permits the retrieval of information that was
not directly stored in it, and retrieval of information leaves its contents unchanged. (1972, p. 385)

Tulving's statement that retrieval from the semantic
(knowledge-based) memory systems leaves its contents unchanged, that semantic memory is not recontextualized, is
an important characteristic that differentiates semantic from
episodic (autobiographical) memory. Episodic memory is
the memory of the self, and apart from trauma, the memory
of the self is continually updated.

Neuroscientists have obtained evidence of neural correlates that confirm Tulving's categories of episodic and semantic memory. Children who sustained bilateral damage
to their hippocampus developed amnesia for autobiographical (episodic) memory, while preserving the memory of acquired knowledge (semantic memory) (Vargha-Khadem,
Gadian, et al. 1997). These researchers infer from their investigation that semantic memory is preserved when the
underlying cerebral cortices are intact. This work also re-
inforces the belief that the hippocampus processes experiential (episodic) memory (Pally 1997). Tulving's distinction
between episodic and semantic memory is also confirmed
by laboratory experiments, as detailed by Daniel Schacter
(1996).

The Recall and Influence of Early Memories

The hippocampus, responsible for declarative memory, is a
structure that is slow to mature, so affective memories from
infancy and early childhood may be retained in the uncon-

scious but cannot be remembered (LeDoux 1996). We know that infantile amnesia persists until about the age of two and a half. But infant researchers can demonstrate that infants remember affective interactions with their caretaker (Beebe, Lachman, et al. 1997). These memories, however, remain implicit; they are what Christopher Bollas (1987) has termed *the unthought known.*

Infant researchers such as Daniel Stern (1994) suggest that infants have a memorial schema consisting of a gestalt of their cognitive and affective interaction with their caretakers, which he calls a "schema of being with." This affective schema is organized along a temporal dimension that can be likened to a narrative. Stern described the interaction as a narrative envelope (I will return to this narrative envelope in chapter 9). The fact that these early memories cannot be made explicit does not mean that they are under repression. It seems likely, therefore, that such early affective memories may be stored as wordless affective metaphors. The amnesia of early childhood thus represents a problem of retrieval of memory rather than registration of memory.

The long-range effect of the unconscious memories of salient interactions between children and their caretakers can be inferred from the so called "dead-mother syndrome" (Green 1986, Modell 1999). Observations from adult psychoanalysis suggest that there are, in some instances, lasting psychological consequences that follow from a child's relationship with a mother who is physically present but emotionally unresponsive. The mother's unresponsiveness is frequently due to the fact that she is significantly depressed. Daniel Stern (1994) described the infant's responses to its depressed mother. He observed the infant's "micro-depression," resulting from its failed attempts to bring a depressed mother back to emotional life. "Compared to the infant's expectations and wishes, the depressed mother's face is flat and expressionless. She breaks eye contact and does not seek to reestablish it. There is less contingent responsiveness."

One has to be cautious in suggesting any invariant or causal connection between maternal care in childhood and later adult psychopathology,[6] as every individual's response to trauma is unique and in health memory is recontextualized. For these reasons, it is difficult to demonstrate with any certainty that there are causal links between patterns of the child's early interaction with its caretakers and later disturbances. Nevertheless, most psychoanalysts believe that the child's interactions with its caretakers are recorded *as potential unconscious memories* that will, in some instances, continue to exert an organizing influence upon adult relationships. I (Modell 1999) and other psychoanalysts have observed that *some* individuals whose mothers were depressed and emotionally unresponsive when they were children are especially vulnerable as adults to states of withdrawal and unrelatedness in those they love. Therefore, it is not unreasonable to assume that patterns of interaction between a young child and its caretakers are unconsciously memorialized and that in some instances such memories can be reevoked and transferred onto present relationships even when the original memories cannot be retrieved.

Comparing the Freudian and Cognitive Unconscious: An Afterthought

As the psychologist Nicholas Humphrey (1997) noted, until Freud the idea of an unconscious mind had been considered a conceptual impossibility. Today Freud's assertion *that mental processes are in themselves unconscious* has been rediscovered by some neuroscientists. For example, Francis Crick and Christof Koch (2000) accept Freud's dictum that thinking is largely unconscious.

Cognitive science now recognizes that consciousness is, as Freud perceived, merely the surface of a mental iceberg in that most cognitive processes, such as procedural memory, are unconscious. It is evident that the Freudian dynamic unconscious and the newly recognized cognitive unconscious represent quite different landscapes. But, I suggest, these landscapes are not entirely incompatible. The Freudian unconscious is implicitly conflictual and dynamic because of the central position given to the fact that repression controls access to consciousness. In the next chapter I will critically examine Freud's concept of repression, which I believe to be a weak link in Freudian theory. But even if we put the concept of repression aside as an explanation, there is unquestionably an involuntary and unconscious selective process that controls access to consciousness. In the Freudian unconscious, conflict is an implicit determinant in deciding what remains unconscious. Freud also believed in a cognitive unconscious, in that he recognized *potential meaning* to be present in unconscious memory. But more important, Freud believed that the unconscious was that part of the mind where man's instinctual endowment made somatic demands upon the self (1940, p. 148). These somatic demands may remain unconscious or be elaborated as conscious images, fantasies, and focused desires.

This aspect of the unconscious is conspicuously absent from recent descriptions of the cognitive unconscious, such as provided by Lakoff and Johnson. They state, "Since cognitive operations are largely unconscious, the term *cognitive unconscious* accurately describes all unconscious mental operations concerned with conceptual systems, meaning and

language" (Lakoff and Johnson 1999, p. 12). They characterize the cognitive unconscious as follows: "The cognitive
unconscious is thoroughly efficacious: intentional, representational, propositional, truth characterizing, inference gen-
erating, imaginative and causal" (1999, p. 117). The
unconscious emotions that dominate the Freudian unconscious are conspicuously absent in this description.

To a psychoanalyst, this is a rather bland, arid, and one-
dimensional view of the unconscious mind as compared to
the Freudian unconscious. The cognitive unconscious must
include an *emotional unconscious,* encompassing not only the
"somatic demands upon the mind" but also the potential
expression of unconscious emotional memory and unconscious fantasy.

3   Imagination's
         Autonomy

All that one can call personality or soul becomes engraved in the nervous system.

Oliver Sacks

The autonomy of imagination is consistent with a view of the brain as a self-activating system (Llinás 2001). Dreaming is a familiar example of such self-activation that expresses the autonomy and uniqueness of an individual's imagination. A dream is quintessentially personal. However, there remains the problem of explaining the dream's self-generated content as the product of a neurophysiological process that is presumably uniform and universal.

Unconscious imagination, dependent upon memory and the metaphoric process, originates as a *personal* unconscious, yet in Freud's topography of the mind, the unconscious is the locus of universal instincts, so that in this sense the Freudian unconscious can be viewed as impersonal. A fantasy, for example, was thought by Freud to be an instinctual derivative. Freud recognized that fantasies were influenced by experience, but to take the Oedipus complex as an example, experience provides only variations on a theme derived from universal instincts. Freud avoided using the term *imagination* and may have done so because it suggests an idiosyncratic creation of the individual. As the philosopher and psychoanalyst Cornelius Castoriadis (1997) cogently noted, Freud did not recognize the significance of the *autonomous* imagination. There is a broader issue at stake here: if the brain is seen as an unstable, self-activating system, can one still think in terms of predictable and universal physiological "mechanisms"?

To explain the translation of instinct into fantasy, Freud relied on a political metaphor. Freud attempted to answer the question of how a process arising from within the body, initiated by instincts or drives, becomes transformed into a product of one's imagination, a fantasy. Fantasy could be explained as a *representation* of the drive. Freud did not use the term *representation,* in the Cartesian sense, to denote a correspondence between objects in the world and their "representation" in the mind. Instead, Freud intended the term to suggest a delegation, representatives of the country of origin. A *representation* would be an intermediary between the domains of psyche and soma (Castoriadis 1987, 1997). A delegation, to extend the metaphor further, must be able to mediate by sharing a common language. The drive must send to the psyche ambassadors that speak a recognizable language. Freud used the metaphor of representation to explain *how matter becomes imagination.* As Francis Crick wrote in *The Astonishing Hypothesis* (1994), "You, your joys and your sorrows, your memories, and your ambitions, your sense of personal identity and free will, are in fact no more than the behavior of a vast assembly of nerve cells and their associated molecules."

The Assumption of a Universal Unconscious Mind

The nineteenth-century romantic movement undoubtedly influenced Freud's conception of a universal unconscious. Lancelot Law Whyte, in *The Unconscious before Freud* (1962), has shown how philosophers, scientists, and poets, beginning in the seventeenth century, contributed to the idea of the unconscious mind. The romantic movement of the nineteenth century believed that the unconscious mind was the underground source through which the individual was able to access the universal forces of nature. Nature, in turn, was seen as a great reservoir of vitality, without which an individual could not remain psychically alive.

Freud incorporated the essence of some of these ideas into his theory of the id. Instincts or drives are impelling forces of nature, shared by all members of our species, that impact upon all individuals' minds through the id. The id, viewed within the topography of the unconscious mind, is the storehouse of those instincts, which reflect the experiences in detail of the human species—a Lamarckian interpretation of evolution. The ego (or self), in contrast, contains the experiences of the individual. Freud believed that his differentiation of the ego from the id represents a fundamental biological distinction between the experience of the individual and the history of the species. If the ego is formed as a result of the interaction of the id with the external world, it rests, as it were, "as a follicle upon the id." The individual, represented by the ego, is not fully autonomous; it is driven by the unconscious id, as portrayed in Freud's famous metaphor of the horse and rider. The ego (self) "has to hold in check the superior strength of the horse; if he is not to be parted, he is obliged to guide it where it wants to go" (Freud 1923a).

I should add, however, that the Freudian unconscious does not consist entirely of the collective, impersonal forces of the id, for Freud also characterized a dynamic, individualized unconscious created by conflict. So the contents of the unconscious mind encompass impersonal instincts as well as specific thoughts and feelings that the individual repressed because of guilt or shame.

In Freudian theory the mechanism of repression explained what remains unconscious. The Greek underworld had a watchdog named Cerberus, who guarded its entrance. For Freud, the watchdog function of Cerberus is assigned to repression, which guards both the exit from and the entrance to the unconscious. The undoing of repression explained the release of thoughts and feelings into consciousness, and Freud attributed such power to words and verbal interpretation. Freud's conception of the unconscious thus placed a high burden of explanation upon the concept of repression, which he conceived of as a psychophysiological mechanism common to all of humanity. I be lieve that such a mechanistic explanation cannot be sustained.

Is Repression a "Mechanism"?

Repression differentiates two levels within the unconscious: the unconscious proper and the preconscious; one inaccessible to consciousness unless repression is lifted, and the other more freely accessible. Freud believed that for unconscious thoughts (in contrast to emotions) to become conscious, they had to be attached to a preconscious system that is both verbal and rational. He believed that for the unconscious to become conscious, thoughts must be connected to verbal memories. In Freud's view, the preconscious system, a linguistic system, is not idiosyncratic; rather, it is a system of shared conventional symbols.

Below is his description of the preconscious as described in *The Interpretation of Dreams* (1900). (Freud had previously explained that the cathectic processes were regulated by releases of pleasure and unpleasure, but that a more subtle and delicate adjustment was necessary when thoughts move toward consciousness.)

For this purpose [for ideas to have access to consciousness apart from strict considerations of pleasure or unpleasure] the PCS [preconscious] system needed to have qualities of its own which could attract consciousness; and it seems highly probable that it obtained them by linking the preconscious processes with the mnemic system of indications of speech, a system not without quality. (Freud 1900, p. 574)

In order that thought-processes may acquire quality [consciousness], they are associated in human beings with verbal memories, whose residues of quality are sufficient to draw attention of consciousness to them and to endow the process of thinking with a new mobile cathexis from consciousness. (Freud 1900, p. 617)

Freud's term *quality* can be traced back to "The project for a scientific psychology" (1895), where it was equated with consciousness.[1] The term *quality* refers to something that is *differentiated,* an essential characteristic of consciousness. In thinking about "quality," Freud was influenced by the assumption, found in the project, that conscious and unconscious thoughts belong not only to separate psychological systems but also to separate neural systems.[2] Freud had equated the unconscious with the passionate, the illogical, and the irrational. In contrast, the preconscious system was seen as logical and orderly. Freud believed that through speech and language one is able to bring logic and rationality to the irrational unconscious, which can do nothing else but wish.

The preconscious is the only mediating agency between the unconscious and consciousness, the only unrestricted route from the unconscious to consciousness. Freud overlooked the role of the autonomous imagination and metaphor in making the unconscious conscious and referred instead to this more impersonal process. As an aside, it is to be regretted that Freud did not develop an idea he shared with Fliess in the letter reproduced in the previous chapter. In that same letter, in which he described memory as a recontextualization (December 6, 1896), he said, "But pathologic defense occurs only against a memory trace from an earlier phase *that has not yet been translated*" (Masson 1985). He never again explained repression as a failure of translation.

One may ask: Why is repression necessary? What is the inner danger that requires repression? Freud believed that the unconscious is a source of danger in itself. It is the intensity of excitation itself that poses a danger to the psyche. If the unconscious erupted unchecked into consciousness, Freud (1900) asserted, the result would be psychosis. Freud also attributed childhood disgust regarding bodily functions as another motive for repression. With regard to the intensity of excitation, he analogized this internal danger to an environmental danger from which the organism takes flight through a withdrawal of cathexis. "The essence of repression lies simply in turning something away, in keeping it at a distance, from the consciousness" (Freud 1915a).[3] As one cannot escape from one's unconscious, our only recourse, according to Freud, is a withdrawal of cathexis. Freud's explanation of repression was essentially based upon an analogy to an organism escaping from external danger, an analogy to the body's attempt to restore homeo-stasis. In this sense, Freud understood repression to be a universal defense mechanism in which individual differ-ences do not make a difference. Repression was explained as a physiological mechanism.

Can we continue to think of repression as a "defense mechanism," an automatic, homeostaticlike process analo-gous to the individual's need to escape from danger, or is repression something that is personal and idiosyncratic? I have come to doubt that there are uniform "defense mecha-nisms." Rather, I think that each one of us responds to pain-ful memories and feelings in his own unique fashion. If this is true, repression should be understood not as a mechanism but as an ad hoc mental construction determined by the con-text of a given experience. *What we fail to remember is also part of our imagination.*

I would not question the existence of the phenomena that repression attempts to explain. No one can doubt that pain-ful thoughts, feelings, and memories that were once con-scious can selectively be lost to consciousness. And it is also true that there is within each of us a very variable resistance to the emergence into consciousness of those banished thoughts, feelings, and memories. What I am suggesting is that each of us has his own style of banishing such un-wanted thoughts and feelings.

The unconscious memory of a "repressed" childhood trauma can sometimes be recovered through psychoanaly-sis, but this is an unusual occurrence. More commonly, the memory of the trauma has remained fully conscious and indeed dominates consciousness (Prager 1998).[4]

What usually has been "repressed" and becomes con-scious in the course of a psychoanalysis are not specific thoughts but the *feeling components* of memories, such as unrecognized love or unrecognized hatred. In addition to the recovery of the feeling components of memories, psychoanalysis may uncover unconscious and disowned aspects of the self, such as one's bisexual or sadistic impulses. We commonly describe these unrecognized or disowned aspects of the self as split off or dissociated from one's sense of personhood. Splitting off or dissociation and repression are usually described as different defense "mechanisms," but instead, these different defense "mechanisms" may simply reflect individual differences.

From a phenomenological point of view, *what* is kept out of consciousness and the *motives* for such "repression" are varied and determined by context. It is unlikely that a universal and unvarying process such as repression can account for unconscious feelings, unconscious memories, and unconscious aspects of the self.

When Do Individual Differences Make a Difference?

My assertion that repression is not a universal "mechanism" illustrates the more widespread and broader problem of using a physiological analogy to explain a psychological process. Freud explained repression as the organism's internal flight from danger. He was implicitly comparing repression to a physiological mechanism associated with what was yet to be called *homeostasis*. (In chapter 5, I will discuss homeostasis, emotions, and the protobiological self as midbrain functions.) At the level of the *biological* self, there may be universal physiological mechanisms. At the more complex level of personhood, individual differences cannot be ignored, and universals analogous to physiological mechanisms become suspect as explanations.

Whether or not individual differences can be bracketed in neuroscience would then depend on whether such global functions as meaning construction are being investigated.[5] It would appear from the enormous success of neurobiology at the levels of molecular and cellular biology that individual differences at these levels can be bracketed and treated as "noise." The selective influence of the self does not enter into individual neurons or synaptic junctions. However, when considering the dynamics of global brain functions, the variations of individual selves will assume greater significance. In neuroscience some methods of investigation mask such individual differences, while others do not. For example, brain-imaging techniques such as fMRI use statistical methods that average out the observations obtained from individual subjects (for a description, see Frackowiak, Friston, et al. 1997). When a different technique is used, such as magnetic encephalography, individual differences, between subjects become apparent. In an experiment that employed magnetic encephalography (MEG) significant differences between individuals were observed. Edelman and Tononi (2000) described the neural correlates of consciousness in an experiment using binocular rivalry. The localities of the brain that coincided with consciousness differed in different subjects. When Walter Freeman (1999b) used the EEG to investigate the rabbit brain's response to odors, he discovered that the pattern of amplitude modulation was unique for each individual rabbit, each rabbit having its own distinctive signature. If rabbits can be said to have imaginations, their imaginations are those of unique individuals.

These findings should not surprise us, for experience sculpts the brain, unlike the liver or kidney. It is now widely recognized that genetic instruction cannot account for the brain's complexity. As Oliver Sacks (1990) observed in his

review of Edelman's contribution, "Our brains create structures in the light of our experiences." Gerald Edelman's Theory of Neuronal Group Selection explains that although the
anatomy of the brain is constrained by genes, connectivity
at the level of synapses is established by somatic selection
during the individual's development, beginning within the
uterus and extending throughout the entire life cycle. The
brains of identical twins are appreciably different. Edelman's theory is a theory of Darwinian selection in somatic
time rather than in evolutionary time. As Sacks (1990) further noted, "Darwin provided a picture of the evolution of
species; Edelman has provided a picture of the evolution of
the individual nervous system, as it reflects life experiences
of each individual human being."

That brains organize essential behaviors not in accordance with a genetic code but as a result of an individual's
trials and errors has been confirmed by investigators of infant motor development. Thelen and Smith (1994) have conclusively demonstrated that each human infant learns to
reach for objects or learns to walk in its own distinct fashion.
Their research demonstrates the uniqueness of individual
solutions to developmental challenges.

Dreaming and the Autonomy of the Imagination

The dream is perhaps the most familiar example of the autonomy of imagination. There may or may not be an unvarying neurophysiological process that creates a dream, but the
result of this neurophysiological process, the remembered
dream, bears the imprint of an individual self. The dream
makes use of the earliest memories of the self and memories
of the previous day. Dream formation remains a puzzle, as
it is, at the same time, an example of the self's autonomous

imagination and the product of a neurophysiological process. How, then, is an impersonal process transformed into the imagination of the dream?

No one has explained the biological function of sleep, and we know even less of the biological function of dreaming. We know that sleep is as necessary to life as is breathing, because sleep deprivation can lead to death. We do not know the effects of prolonged dream deprivation. Neuroscientists Borbély and Tononi (1998, p. 212) suggest that sleep and dreaming reorganize and reactivate patterns of brain activity experienced during waking. They believe that only the activity of the *waking conscious* brain (Freud's day residue) is reorganized. However, there is little agreement regarding the nature of the reorganization that takes place during sleep. Some hypothesize that sleep is a time for restoration, while others view sleep as a time for stimulation. These two processes may not prove to be contradictory, for stimulation may prove to be restorative.

The philosopher Owen Flanagan (2000) has called dreams the "spandrels of sleep," an evolutionary side effect of no biological significance in itself. *Spandrel* is an architectural term that Stephen Jay Gould used as a metaphor to describe the nonadaptive side effects that are by-products of evolution. Gould (2000) describes spandrels as the triangular space that is "left over" between a rounded arch and the rectangular frame of wall and ceiling. He adds that such by-products may be co-opted for useful purposes. Flanagan would claim that dreams serve no biological function but nonetheless can be put to good use in expanding self-knowledge, which is, of course, the traditional use that psychoanalysis has made of dreams.

In a recent experiment using rats, Kenway Louie and Matthew Wilson (2001) observed that the same pattern of neural activity in the hippocampus that accompanied a repeated daytime task (finding food in a circular run) appeared during REM sleep. The hippocampus is the locus for the organization of spatial memory in the rat. As I shall shortly note, there is some reason to question the reliability of REM sleep as a marker of dreams. We cannot be certain that these rats were dreaming in REM sleep, but this research demonstrated that during sleep (whether in the dream state or not) there is a replay and probable reorganization of the memories of intentional acts, memories acquired during the waking state of the previous day. Rats as well as humans respond to what Freud called the "day's residue."

The research of Mark Solms, who is both a neuropsychologist and a psychoanalyst, has challenged the conventional understanding of the neurobiology of dreaming. Correlating the remembered dreams of brain-damaged patients, Solms (1997a, 1997b, 1999) has demonstrated that it is a process within the forebrain, and not the primitive brain stem, that generates the dream. Solms' investigation of 332 patients suffering from brain lesions has demonstrated a double dissociation between REM sleep and dreaming. He has shown that dreams are generated from the neocortex and not the brain stem. He has also shown that patients who have lesions that abolish REM asleep go on dreaming, while patients with damage to the neocortex have their dreams extinguished. Dreams may be activated in tandem with REM sleep, but there is no simple causal relationship. Solms' research has conclusively demonstrated that REM sleep cannot be used with any confidence as a marker of dreams. As we are the only animal that can report dreams, animal research that infers dreaming from REM sleep becomes questionable.[6] But as yet Solms' research has had hardly any impact on the community of dream investigators. We cannot know whether other animals are also conscious of their dreams, but we can be sure that our distinctive cognitive capacities make our own dreams unique.

Solms' findings are consistent with those of Panksepp (1998a), who reported an earlier study of lobotomized patients. These individuals with damaged forebrains demonstrated the physiological signs of REM sleep but did not dream.

I believe that there are significant individual differences in the *uses* made of the dreaming process, which means that it will not be possible to generalize about the function of *all* dreams. Freud has been justly criticized for proclaiming that all dreams are wish fulfillments. Some dreams undoubtedly are wish fulfillments, or to state it in a different terminology, some dreams reflect an unconscious intentionality. If there are significant individual differences in the uses made of dreams and if dreams serve different functions during different nights, it is possible that on a given night a dream may not indicate an unconscious intentionality but be simply a processing of the memorial inputs of the previous day.

Tucker and Luu (1998) offer such a hypothesis. Freud thought of the day residue, those events of the preceding day that evoked the dream, as an entrepreneur who needed the venture capital of the unconscious wish to create a dream. Tucker and Luu offer an alternative possibility. The day residue provides a novel experience that requires the entire memory system to be readjusted. (Louie and Wilson's investigations of possibly dreaming rats, which I cited earlier, would support this hypothesis.) Tucker and Luu view the function of dreaming as a consolidation of memory, which involves an interleaving of new patterns with existing connections. They state, "To the extent that new synaptic connection weights must convolve recent experience with remote memories, the entire contents of past memory, at least those that are to be retained, would need to be activated during the consolidation process" (1998). In this fashion the random sensory events of waking life are reorganized in accordance with the history of the self.

Freud's Specimen Dream of the Botanical Monograph

Freud's dream of the Botanical Monograph remains one of the best illustrations of the dream as an unconscious metaphoric process. Freud did not directly identify what we now recognize to be metaphor. Freud instead characterized as *condensation* the superimposition of dream thoughts and images.[7] He may have further obscured the significance of unconscious metaphor in dreams, for he also mistakenly thought that certain dream images could be decoded in accordance with a universal and impersonal symbolism, which, if true, would negate the dream's idiosyncratic meaning. If the dream could be decoded using elements of a universal symbolism, this would deny the existence of an autonomous imagination. This fundamental contradiction and inconsistency in Freud's *Interpretation of Dreams* is discussed at some length in Rand and Torok's *Questions for Freud* (1997).

When Freud interpreted certain dream elements as conventional symbols, he unsuspectingly illustrated the difference between metaphor and symbol. A symbol has a fixed referent determined by convention, whereas metaphor has no fixed referent. There are, of course, conventional or worn-out metaphors, but that is usually not the stuff that dreams are made of. The unconscious metaphoric process of the dream is autonomous, but this does not exclude the possibility that a dream may make use of conventional symbols. In any case, there is no standard interpretation of dream images. This distinction between the individual's imagination and conventional symbolism reminds me of Samuel Taylor Coleridge's critical analysis of poetry. Coleridge (1817) contrasted the author's ready-made, conventional associations, which he described as "fancy," with the poet's true autonomous imagination.

This is one version of the dream of the Botanical Monograph. Three slightly different versions of the dream appear in *The Interpretation of Dreams*, which suggests that this dream was one that was especially significant for Freud (for further discussion of this point, see Anzieu 1986).

I had written a monograph on a certain plant. *The book lay before me* and I was at that moment turning over a folded colored plate. Bound up in each copy there was a dried specimen of the plant, as though it had been taken from a herbarium. (Freud 1900, p. 169)

On the night before, Freud received a letter from Wilhelm Fliess: "I am very much preoccupied with your dream-book. *I see it lying finished before me.* I see myself turning over its pages."[8] That morning, preceding the dream, Freud had seen a new book on the genus Cyclamen in the window of a book shop. Freud recounts a further day residue of the dream. During the same evening he had a long conversation with his friend Königstein regarding a Festschrift that omitted reference to Freud's contribution to the discovery of the anesthetic properties of cocaine. Freud's conversation with his friend also included an allusion to a patient of Freud's called Flora and a friend of his wife, Frau L., who had met Freud's wife Martha two days before the dream and whom he had treated some years earlier. Frau L. had been accustomed to receiving a bouquet of flowers from her husband on her birthday, and once, he forgot, causing her to burst into tears. Freud thought of his own failure as a husband, for Cyclamen was Martha's favorite flower, which he also neglected to bring her. A further botanical reference in the events preceding the dream is that when Freud was conversing with his friend Königstein, he was joined by a Professor Gärtner (the German for gardener).

Freud's associations to his dream also included a revealing fantasy or daydream: "If ever I get glaucoma, I thought, I should travel to Berlin to get myself operated on incognito, in my friend's [Fliess's] house, by a surgeon recommended by him. The operating surgeon, who would have no idea of my identity, would boast once again of how easily such operations could be performed since the introduction of cocaine; and I should not give the slightest hint that I myself had a share in the discovery" (Freud 1900, p. 170).

This pleasurable fantasy was also accompanied by associations of an opposite nature, memories of failure in school as a child, a rare event for Freud. As a young student he did poorly in botany and failed to identify a specimen of a plant.

As a further association of this dream, Freud cited the following selection from Goethe's *Faust*:

A thousand threads one treadle throws,
Where fly the shuttles hither and thither,
Unseen the threads are knit together,
And an infinite combination grows.

These few lines can be interpreted as a description of the unconscious metaphoric process that weaves and synthesizes disparate elements. The wish for the appearance of the completed master work that will assure his fame is woven together with opposite thoughts of inadequacy, failure, and the absence of recognition such as occurred in the cocaine episode. Dream condensation, the unconscious metaphoric process, creates a mosaic of layered interrelated meanings. So when one selects one element, it says nothing about other possible interpretations. In accordance with the theme of failure and inadequacy, some commentators on the dream of the Botanical Monograph have interpreted the "dried specimen" as a metaphor for Freud's fear of a waning sexual and creative potency (Anzieu 1986).

The botanical associations that preceded the dream and that Freud described as the day residues—the sight of the monograph on Cyclamen, hearing about the woman Flora, meeting Professor Gärtner—are all metonymic associations, concrete and literal, and lack the synthetic quality of metaphor.

The linguist Roman Jakobson (1995) also observed that metaphor and metonymy contributed to the dream process but are always antagonistically linked.[9] Jakobson believes that metonymic associations explain the dream work that Freud described as *displacement.* The concept of displacement refers to the distinction between manifest and latent dream elements. The manifest elements of the dream—in this instance, plants, flowers, and botanical specimens—have in themselves little to do with the true subject matter of the dream—Freud's career and his hopes for the fame that will follow from *The Interpretation of Dreams.* The deeper meaning of the dream resides elsewhere, yet the metonymic associations form a linked network of their own. Jakobson viewed metonymy as a kind of contiguity, prevalent in magical thought, where the part stands for the whole. He further believed that prose, in contrast with poetry, is forwarded essentially by contiguity: "Thus for poetry, metaphor, and for prose, metonymy" (Jakobson 1995).

The Dream Wish and Unconscious Intentionality

As in waking life, past, present, and future time are represented in a dream, but the dreamer is only conscious of the present time of the dream narrative. The past in the dream remains unconscious, and the memories enlisted by the dream may refer to the immediate past, as represented by images from the previous day, or the distant past of childhood. If the dream is an expression of intentionality, there is an implicit reference to the future, which may take the form of reference to actions to be taken on the following day or in the more distant future.

Thomas Aquinas defined an *intent* as action toward some future goal that is defined and chosen by the actor. An unconscious dream wish, as a potential action, would satisfy this definition and could be taken as an expression of intentionality. Sleep researchers Greenberg, Katz, et al. (1992) have demonstrated that dreams are problem solving and represent an attempt to adapt to the demands of life experiences. We should not forget that Freud dreamt his Botanical Monograph dream in 1898, when he was working to complete his book on dreams. It can be safely assumed that the dream of the Botanical Monograph was dreamt for *The Interpretation of Dreams.* That is to say, the dream of the Botanical Monograph reflects an unconscious intent to dream a dream that would serve as a confirmatory illustration for *The Interpretation of Dreams.* This does not negate the validity of Freud's associations to the dream; it merely indicates that he needed this dream for his career and to allay his fears of nonrecognition. The dream wish represented an intended action in the world.

Something similar occurs when patients in psychoanalysis dream dreams for the analysis itself, in anticipation of the events of the following day, when the dream will be recounted to the analyst. For a patient in analysis, dreams are seldom, if ever, impersonal "noise"; they are invariably self-referential and intentional. When there is a positive relationship with the analyst and when resistance to the work tends to be diminishing, dreams may be rich in meaning and relatively accessible to interpretation. Conversely, analysts are well acquainted with the so-called "resistance dream," which tends to be long winded and difficult, if not impossible, to interpret.

To summarize, the unconscious intentionality of dreams may include a "snapshot" that reflects the dreamer's internal psychic state of the preceding day. This repeats an observation that W. R. D. Fairbairn made 50 years ago. He said, "Dreams are essentially not wish fulfillments, but dramatizations or 'shorts' [in the cinematographic sense] of situations existing in inner reality" (Fairbairn 1952). The dream may be a warning message from a split-off part of the dreamer's self. Dreams may anticipate a problem or task that the following day will present. Or the intentionality of the dream may be, as Freud believed, to preserve sleep. A familiar example of the wish to preserve sleep is the urination dream, in which the dreamer, in response to a full bladder, dreams that he is urinating.

Dreaming cannot be explained by reference to a single psychological function. There is an enormous variability in the use that an individual will make of the dream process. Some dreams may reflect unconscious intentionality, while others, as some have claimed, may be merely the neurophysiological "noise" that accompanies the retranscription of the previous day's memories. These dreams may represent the by-products of a reintegration of memory. Each one of us may dream in our own particular way, and the use we make of dreaming will differ during different nights, depending on what remains to be processed from the previous day's experiences. This makes it impossible to assign a single, uniform function to dreaming.

We should also be aware of the danger of confusing the meaning of a dream with the function of dreaming. Searching for the neural correlates of dream censorship and assuming that there are neural correlates that would differentiate the manifest and latent content of a dream seem to me to be misplaced. For example, some neuroscientists (Braun 1999) claim that dreams have no latent content but only manifest content. Differentiating between latent and manifest content can be demonstrated in Freud's dream of the Botanical Monograph, but it requires psychological free association (either that of Freud himself or that of the reader). It is an explanation that is possible only at the level of psychology and does not translate into neurophysiology. We should not expect to find neural correlates of manifest and latent dream thoughts or of dream censorship. It is only for the *process* of dreaming that we may expect to find an explanation in neurophysiology.

4   The Corporeal Imagination

The body creates its sensations; therefore there is a corporeal imagination.

Cornelius Castoriadis

We are not the only species to use our bodies to create meaning. Nonhuman primates such as pygmy chimpanzees and howler monkeys can make use of bodily gestures as iconic signs. Observers report, "When approaching a male, the female howler in estrus will form an oval opening with her lips and her protruding tongue will rapidly oscillate in and out and up and down. It is clear to the observer that the function of this gesture is to invite copulation" (Sheets-Johnstone 1984). These nonhuman primates use their bodies as we also do, as a *semantic template.* In this chapter I intend to demonstrate that *the body is both the initial source and the sustaining source of an autonomous imagination.*

As I have described in chapter 2, emotional memories form categories based on metaphoric similarity. Metaphor is thus the interpreter of unconscious memory. Inasmuch as consciousness is simultaneously directed toward the external world and the interior of the body, bodily sensations

are the counterpart of perception. I will suggest that sensations arising from the interior of our body are subject to the
same metaphoric transformations as are sensations arising
from the external world. In this sense we can speak of a
corporeal imagination. Freud's libido theory may be anti-
quated, but it is nevertheless instructive when reinterpreted
not as a reflection of instinct but as an unconscious metaphoric process. A broader cognitive theory of emotion will
need to recognize this uniquely human aspect of the interpretation of feeling due to our capacity for metaphoric
thought. (I will enlarge on this topic in chapter 7.)

The Bodily Sources of Metaphor

Metaphor has been defined as the transfer of meaning
between dissimilar domains. In the previous chapters I
described how, in the case of traumatic memories, a metaphoric process transfers meaning between the dissimilar domains of past and present time. In this chapter I shall
describe the transfer of meaning, not between past and present time, but between different sensory modalities.

The neurologist Norman Geschwind (1965) investigated
the neural correlates of cross-modal mapping. He placed
this process within an evolutionary perspective when he proposed that such cross-modal mappings are automatic and
involuntary in nonhuman primates. Geschwind observed
that nonhuman primates, in contrast to human beings,
are able to form cross-modal associations but only if such
associations are linked to the limbic system, that is to say,
are emotionally driven. He suggested that if cross-modal
associations are freed from an involuntary coupling with homeostatic needs, this would also facilitate the emergence of

higher-order mental processes, such as language. A further implication is that in humans, cross-modal associations, linked with higher cognitive processes, can go "offline" and be freed from the tyranny of environmental inputs.

The earliest experience of what might be called a proto-metaphor may be found in the infant's perception of cross-modal matching between the major sensory portals of sight, hearing, kinesthesia, and touch. We know that infants and young children are delighted when the narrative of a nursery rhyme or song is accompanied by mimetic gestures: infants experience the transfer of meaning between different sensory domains as inherently pleasurable. Thelen and Smith in *A Dynamic Systems Approach to the Development of Cognition and Action* (1994) review the considerable evidence for cross-modal performance in infancy. By one month, infants match the oral feel and sight of textured pacifiers. Infants at three months learn to integrate and coordinate information from many sensory modalities. Mobiles are seen as well as kicked, rattles are shook as well as heard, dolls are sucked as well as felt, and so on. Four-month-old infants prefer to watch complex visual events that match ongoing complex auditory events. Many experiments demonstrate that infants can easily match puppets, sponges, and blocks with their appropriate sounds. Cross-modal matchings are the norm in infancy.

Cross-modal matchings also characterize the infant's sensuous experience of their mother. So cross-modal matching is associated with the infant's first experiences of intersubjectivity. Daniel Stern (1985) recognized that for infant/mother emotional attunement to work, the infant must have this capacity for cross-modal perception. He said, "If a certain gesture by the mother is to be 'correspondent' with a certain vocal exclamation by the infant, the two expressions must share some common currency that permits them to be transferred from one modality or form to another" (Stern 1985, p. 152). From these early affective communications between mother and infant, we may infer that the infant is compelled, within the context of maternal bonding, to discover equivalent meaning across different sensory portals.

The infant perceives the mother's feelings by seeing, especially the mother's face and eyes, hearing her tone of voice, feeling her touch, and kinesthetic sensations, including posture and muscular tension. The infant feels pleasure or discomfort in the interior of its body, and this is communicated to the mother through these multiple sensory and motoric channels. The mother, in turn, responds to the infant's communication by modifying her tone of voice, facial expression, and bodily musculature. Sensory experiences of mother and infant are conjoined through cross-modal matching.

Stern points out that this capacity of the infant to find equivalent meaning across different sensory modalities helps to explain the intersubjective process of affective attunement between mother and child. This is a dialogue, moving together in time, that occurs long before the acquisition of verbal language, and this suggests a profound connection between feeling and metaphor.

It is therefore not unreasonable to suppose that the infant's capacity to create perceptual metaphors appears early in development, and that conceptual metaphor is not very far behind. The use of conceptual metaphor has been observed in children around 18 months of age. For example, Lakoff and Johnson (1999) report that toddlers demonstrate conceptual metaphors by conflating two sensory domains, such as seeing and knowing. Toddlers also show the capacity to use space metaphorically: nearness stands for similarity and farness stands for dissimilarity (cited by Thelen and Smith 1994).

Psychoanalyst Susan Isaacs (1948) described the following case:

A little girl of one year and eight months, with poor speech development, saw a shoe of her mother's from which the sole had become loose and was flopping about. The child was horrified and screamed with terror. For about a week she would shrink away and scream if she saw her mother wearing any shoes at all, and for some time could only tolerate her mother's wearing a pair of brightly colored house shoes. The particular offending pair was not worn for several months. The child gradually forgot about the terror, and let her mother wear any sort of shoes. At two years 11 months, however (15 months later), she said suddenly to her mother in a frightened voice: "Where are Mommy's broken shoes?" Her mother hastily said, fearing another screaming attack, that she had sent them away, and the child then commented: "They might have eaten me right up." The flapping shoe was thus seen by the child as a threatening mouth and responded to it as such.

There is little doubt that this 20-month-old child reacted to a perceptual metaphor that originated from her own bodily experience of eating things up. This experience found its mirror counterpart in the mother's mouth, and through animistic projection, her mother's shoe became a living object.

Synesthesia

Synesthesia was observed in the eighteenth century. John Locke in his *Essay Concerning Human Understanding* (1689, p. 276) relates that a studious blind man bragged one day that he now understood what *scarlet* signified. When his friend asked what scarlet is, the blind man answered that it is the sound of a trumpet. Synesthesia, a relatively rare neuropsychological condition, is an exaggerated form of cross-modal mapping in which the individual may "hear" colors or, seeing the color red, may detect the "scent" of red as well. Synesthesia is of interest as it illustrates a form of involuntary cross-modal mapping, a type of involuntary perceptual metaphor. That some great artists have been synesthetes suggests that a neural predisposition may lead to the creation of novel metaphors.

The neurologist Richard Cytowic (1993) reported the case of "a man who tasted shapes." This synesthete explained that flavors have shapes and that when cooking a chicken, he "wanted the taste of the chicken to be a pointed shape but it came out round." There have been well-known poets and musicians who were synesthetes, such as Scriabin, Vasily Kandinsky, and perhaps best known, Baudelaire. Vladimir Nabokov in his autobiography *Speak Memory* (1989) reveals that he too is a synesthete, which he describes as a case of "colored hearing": "The long *a* of the English alphabet has for me the tint of weathered wood; the French *a* evokes polished ebony. This black group also includes hard *g* (vulcanized rubber) and *r* (a sooty bag being ripped)." Nabokov's "colored hearing" undoubtedly contributed to his remarkable linguistic sensitivity.

The linguist Roman Jakobson (1995) observed that "free standing" phonemes have synesthetic properties. An example he cited is "the tense /u/ in English words that suggest foolishness—rube, boob, nincompoop, stooge, goof, etc." He further noted that these semantic-sound parallelisms move on an unconscious level. Jakobson observed that there is a polarity between "light" and "dark" vowels that enhances the contrast between the Latin *dies* (day) and *nox* (night). *Dies* sounds lighter than *nox.* Jakobson quoted the art historian Gombrich, who wrote, "It is my conviction that the problem of synesthetic equivalences will cease to look embarrassingly arbitrary and subjective if we fix our attention not on likeness of elements but on structural relationships within a scale or matrix. When we say that *u* is dark blue and *i* is bright green, we are talking playful nonsense. But when I say that *i* is brighter than *u*, we find a surprising degree of general consent. I think that the majority would agree that the step from *u* to *i* is more like an upward step than a downward step" (Gombrich 1960, p. 370).

In our experience of music and visual art we take synesthesia for granted. This is evident in so-called program music, where visual scenes are represented aurally. Susanne Langer (1967) was one of the first to note the significance of such cross-modal "sensuous" metaphors in all forms of art. One thinks, for example, of Mussorgsky's musical depiction of a visual scene, *Pictures at an Exhibition,* or Mendelssohn's *Fingal Cave Overture,* describing an actual cave in the Hebrides. There are also reverse examples where something visual portrays an auditory experience, such as Mondrian's "Broadway Boogie-Woogie" (Gombrich 1960).

Lakoff and Johnson's Hypothesis of Primary Metaphor

You will recall that Vico wrote (and I quote again), "It is noteworthy that in all languages the greater part of the expressions relating to inanimate things are formed by metaphor from the human body and its parts and from the human senses and passions." Vico knew nearly 250 years ago that metaphors are generated from the sensations, sounds, and feelings arising from and within the human body, which are then projected outward onto inanimate things. This fact has recently been rediscovered by cognitive linguistics. We unconsciously create metaphors from sensory inputs arising within the body. We form fundamental cognitive tools as the result of a metaphoric process that transfers meaning between different sensory domains. George Lakoff and Mark Johnson (1999) describe these bodily metaphors as primary.

One such primary metaphor is that of verticality and balance. Maintaining an upright posture is a universal developmental achievement of early childhood. This achievement of verticality is accompanied by a sense of balance. Both verticality and balance are felt to be "good." The kinesthetic sensation of verticality, preserving an up-down posture in space against the pull of gravity, is mapped or projected onto abstract conceptual domains far removed from the original kinesthetic bodily experience. These primary metaphors result in the universal assumption that *up* means an increase in quantity and *down* the reverse. Stock markets go both up and down. Some substances are "uppers" and some are "downers," which implies that up is "good" and down is "bad." Feeling good means things are "looking up," and feeling bad means things are "looking down." There is no logical reason why an increase in quantity or the values good and bad should be associated with verticality. As Johnson (1987) observes, this metaphor is so basic to how we organize experience that it seems odd to question it.

Johnson (1987) explained that the transfer of meaning, the process of mapping from bodily experience to abstract concepts, requires the formation of an intermediate image schema. An image schema is not an image but a hypothetical process that produces a product such as a linguistic metaphor. Johnson defines an image schema as "a recurring dynamic pattern of our perceptual interactions and motor programs that give coherence and structure to our experience" (1987, p. xiv). Johnson notes that the key word here is *structure*—there can be no meaning without some form of structure that establishes relationships.[1] So implicit in the metaphors of verticality and balance is an organizing image schema.

The toddler who is able to achieve an upright posture does so because she has developed a sense of balance. To quote Johnson,

The experience of balance is so pervasive and so absolutely basic for our coherent experience of our world, and our survival in it, that we are seldom ever aware of its presence. We almost never reflect on the nature and meaning of balance, and yet without it our physical reality would be nearly chaotic, like the wildly spinning world of a very intoxicated person. The structure of balance is one of the key threads that holds our physical experience together as a relatively coherent and meaningful whole. And balance, metaphorically interpreted also holds together several aspects of our understanding of the world. (1987, p. 74)

We know that the organizing schema of balance is mapped onto diverse and totally unrelated domains, such as the visual arts, music, jurisprudence, intellectual reasoning, mental health, and so forth. We may experience a painting or sculpture as balanced, but the sense of balance resides in ourselves, in our cognitive processes, and not in the painting or sculpture. To believe that balance resides in the object and not in ourselves is an illusion that we construct and an illusion that is very difficult for us to recognize.[2] This metaphoric transfer of the balance schema clearly shows that metaphor is an integral part of cognitive processing. As Lakoff and Johnson (1999) demonstrate, this kind of metaphorization is fundamentally a centrifugal process arising in the body and spreading outwards into the world; the bodily self is projected onto the world.

The body as a container is another primary metaphor that originates from bodily sensations. The sense of boundedness is one of the most pervasive features of our bodily experience. Unlike the metaphor of balance, which maps onto a multitude of abstract concepts, including the mind, the container metaphor makes special reference to the mind.

Mark Johnson states, "We are immediately aware of our bodies as three-dimensional containers into which we put certain things (food, water, air) and out which other things emerge (wastes, air, blood, etc.). From the beginning, we experience constant physical containment in our surroundings (those things that envelope us). We move in and out of rooms, clothes, vehicles, and numerous kinds of bounded spaces" (1987, p. 21).

This pervasive kinesthetic experience of our body moving in space provides a containment schema consisting of a boundary, distinguishing an interior from an exterior, and having contents. This kinesthetic body schema of contained substances moving in and out becomes an organizing metaphor for feelings and theories of mind. The mind has contents. Psychoanalysts have long recognized that unspoken words can be metaphorized as concrete objects in the interior of the body, and as such can be equated with bodily contents (Sharpe 1940). Thus a sudden outpouring of speech was (in the Victorian era) linguistically equated with an ejaculation. Feelings can also be metaphorized as concrete substances within a closed container. The heightened intensity of an affective experience is then felt as a pressure within the container. The physiologic effects of emotion, such as the sensations of flushing and bodily heat, embellish the metaphoric schema. Lakoff provides numerous examples:

"His pent-up anger *welled up* inside him; she got all *steamed up;* I could barely *contain* my rage" (1987, p. 384).

Inchoate feelings require organizing metaphors. Intense feelings, whether it be rage or sexual desire, may be felt as a hot pressure within the body seeking escape, seeking to escape from the body as a container. Feelings are the contents of the container, substances under pressure, as if the pressure of the feeling would threaten the container itself with disruption and disintegration. Our language is replete with clichéd metaphors derived from this generic schema. For example, one is *bursting* with desire; if angry, one may be about to *blow one's top;* and so forth. The fact that intense feelings both erotic and aggressive are intrinsically out of our control, leads to a metaphoric association between uncontrollable feelings (the contents of the mind) and the idea of going crazy. *Out of control* can map on to the metaphor of a fracture in the container, which is the self. A patient who believed that to love is dangerous because of the pressure of feelings felt as if her love were like a dammed up reservoir—if the floodgates were opened, she would lose control, and her very self would fracture, disintegrate, and be swept away. For the same reason, some patients fear the uncontrolled intense delight of orgasm because the uncontrolled feelings are felt to be dangerous in that they threaten to rupture the container.

We take for granted the primary metaphor that our body/self is a container into which we place "good" substances and expel noxious substances. As our sense of self is fundamentally a bodily self, we *are* this container, and the "good" that we take in is then unconsciously mapped on to our feelings of self-worth. If one is in a good mood, what is good is inside the self, and what is bad may be placed outside of the self. In this primitive evaluation, the non-me is bad. This bodily metaphor underlies the defense of projection. Or these values can be reversed, for we also know that when one is depressed, the "good" contents of the self can turn worthless and noxious.

Inasmuch as this image schema of the body has two openings—one that takes in what is good and another that expels what is bad—the self can be purified by ridding itself of its noxious contents. For example, a bulimic patient believed that what is vomited out is the disgusting contents of the self and what remains inside is pure, smooth, and clean.

The psychoanalyst Wilfred Bion (1972) used the metaphor of *the container and the contained* to conceptualize the mutual process of affect regulation that occurs in infancy between mother and child. He believed that the mother could process the infant's anxiety and then feed it back to her in a less toxic form. The (healthy) mother's self is a more effective container as compared to the child's immature self. This metaphor of the container and the contained is consistent with the schema of the body as formulated by Johnson, but now we add the important extension that this primary metaphor derives not only from the sensations of a single body, but also from bodies *in interaction with each other*. This process of mutual affect regulation is frequently referred to as affect containment. This is a further example of how the container metaphor pervades our thinking about the mind.

Unconscious Guilt and the Body as a Container

As a clinician I have learned that the metaphor of the body as a container is at the heart of certain pathogenic fantasies that are nearly impossible to transform. These fantasies can be justifiably called malignant. Some years ago I observed such an elemental fantasy that for many people can be a source of unconscious guilt (Modell 1965). The primary metaphor of the body as a container leads to the following image: *when something "good" is taken into the body/self, it is "all gone" and taken away and not available to other members of the family.* The transformative and generative power of metaphor is such that it can expand this primary metaphor into an organizing schema with innumerable variations. For example, the "good" thing taken into the body may be equated with mother's milk, with being loved, or with possessing some *good,* such as a notable talent or high intelligence. Or the "good" that one has acquired may simply be having a more benign fate than other members of the family. All of this is an elaboration of the bodily metaphor that what is "good" is ingested or in some fashion incorporated into the body / self and therefore is taken away and not available to others. The individual who possesses this "good" consequently feels guilty, because they have taken away something of value from others in the family. Having something "good" within one's self may lead to a kind of survivor guilt. The individual compares his good fortune to the current fate of other family members and feels guilty if the balance of "good" is in his favor. This unconscious fantasy of the body as a container may lead to the belief that one needs to justify one's existence and that ultimately one does not have a right to a life (Modell 1965).

Possessing something good may also lead to the thought that taking away what is "good" harms others. If other family members, such as siblings, are in fact harmed by illness or other misfortunes of fate, the subject's guilt will be that much increased. Some people have the fantasy that becoming separate and autonomous will harm their mothers. Again, this can be understood as a variation on the basic schema that the "good" is experienced as a content within the container of the self. In becoming a separate person, one takes away "good" contents from the mother's self, one deprives the mother of her internal substance and consequently depletes the mother and harms her. A woman patient, for example, was convinced that her mother's illness was caused by her emigrating to a foreign country. Had she remained at home, she was convinced, her mother would not be ill. Metaphors can be dangerous when they become real.

It can be seen then that such bodily metaphors cast a very wide net, with innumerable variations on this common theme. If one believes that one has acquired a good at the expense of other family members, one may feel irrationally responsible for the misfortune of others. In another example, an unmarried woman grew up in a family in which there was both a death of a sibling and a father's deteriorating illness. She felt that she could not have anything for herself. This guilt interfered with her relationships with men. For if she became aware of the man's pain and suffering, she then could not make any claims or demands for herself, and as a consequence she avoided intimate relationships.

Bodily Metaphors Provide an Illusion of Constancy in the Midst of Change

Creating a sense of stability in the midst of the chaos of the physical world is recognized as a general feature of our mind/brain. Because time's arrow never stands still, the context of our experiences is never *precisely the same.* The mind/brain makes comparisons and searches for similarities, and this contributes to the illusion of constancy. In the construction of meaning, there is a sense of safety in the familiar.

Although visual perception is quite different from the construction of meaning, an analogy can be found in the neurophysiology of color perception. The neurophysiologist Semir Zeki (1993) has shown that our subjective experience of color as a constant property in the world is an illusion. Because we view objects under different conditions of illumination, the wavelength composition of light reflected from these objects constantly changes. The constancy of our subjective experience of a color results from a comparison that occurs within the brain. The brain compares the wavelength composition from the light that is reflected from a surface and the wavelength composition of the light reflected from surrounding surfaces. The neurophysiology of color, an unconscious process, is therefore a comparison of comparisons.

It may be the role of somatic metaphors, through the creation of an equivalence of meaning, to create an illusion of constancy. Metaphor then provides a bridge between disconnected experiences. The body, through the use of metaphor, creates somatic templates. I will suggest that Freud's *libido theory* is based on such somatic metaphors. Freud attributed libidinal continuity to what he thought to be a fact of nature, instinctual entities, whereas I am suggesting that the sense of libidinal continuity is something that we create for ourselves.

When discrete experiences are welded together, we think of them as developmentally continuous. Metaphor then contributes to the illusion not only of the constancy of the self (in current time) but also to the continuity of the self through time past. Inasmuch as metaphor is the means by which we find the familiar in something unfamiliar, metaphor is a necessary cognitive component in maintaining a sense of the continuity of our bodily selves.[3]

Libido Theory as a Form of Corporeal Imagination

Freud believed libido theory explained the continuity and transformation of erotic sensations and feelings. In tracing the development of sexuality in the child, Freud identified well-known privileged erotic zones—including the mouth, the skin, the anus, and the genitals—that are developmentally united through the transformations of libido. What Freud attributes to libidinal continuity, I suggest is made possible by means of an unconscious metaphoric process that interprets and transforms sensations. Although Freud never mentioned metaphor, as we shall see, Freud essentially described such a metaphoric process.

Freud observed the transfer *of equivalent meaning* that results from the sensations aroused by different bodily openings, such as lips, vagina, and anus. This lead to Freud's describing the transfer of meaning among *baby, feces,* and *penis.* He wrote, "Feces, penis and baby are all three solid bodies; they all three, by forcible entry or expulsion, stimulate a membranous passage, i.e., the rectum and the vagina, the latter being, as it were, 'taken on lease' from the rectum" (Freud 1917, p. 133). He stated, *"In the psychical sphere an organic correspondence reappears as an unconscious identity"* (my emphasis). This "unconscious identity" we can now interpret as a metaphoric identity.

Freud provides additional examples of metaphoric equivalences in his *New Introductory Lectures:*

The anus corresponds to the primitive mouth, which has migrated down the end of the bowel. We have learnt, then, that after a person's own feces, his excrement, has lost its value for him, this instinctual interest derived from the anal source passes over onto objects that can be presented as *gifts.* And this is rightly so, for feces were the first gift that an infant could make, something he could part with out of love, for whoever was looking after him. Corresponding exactly to analogous changes of meaning that occur in linguistic development, this ancient interest in feces is transformed into the high valuation of *gold* and *money*, but also makes a contribution to the affective cathexis of *baby* and *penis*. It is a universal conviction among children, who long retain the cloaca theory, that babies are born from the bowel like a piece of feces: defecation is the model of the active birth. But the penis has its forerunner in the column of feces which fills and stimulates the mucous membranes of the bowel. When a child, unwillingly enough, comes to realize that there are human creatures who do not possess a penis, that organ appears to him as something detachable from the body and becomes unmistakably analogous to the excrement, which was the first piece of bodily material that had to be renounced. A great part of anal eroticism is thus carried over into a cathexis of the penis. But the interest in that part of the body has, in addition to its anal-erotic root, an oral one which is perhaps more powerful still: for when sucking has come to an end, the penis also becomes heir to the mothers nipple. If one is not aware of these profound connections, it is impossible to find one's way about in the fantasies of human beings, influenced as they are by the unconscious. Feces, money, gifts, baby, penis are treated [in the unconscious] as though they meant the same thing. (1933b, pp. 100–101)

This displacement of affective interest that Freud describes from the mother's nipple to the penis and from feces to gifts and money is made possible by means of unconscious metaphor. It is this singularly human capacity for an autonomous corporeal imagination that makes the concepts of instincts and unitary drives so unsatisfactory. Although Freud distinguished what he called *Trieb* (drive) from animal *Instinkt* (instinct), he viewed both drive and instinct as psychobiological entities, the building blocks of his theory. Freud explained the evident variability of instinctual manifestations by positing that the libido had different aims and objects. For example, Freud thought of sublimation as a transformation of energy, as a kind of "deinstinctualiza-tion." Although Freud described the transformative aspects of instinct, he could not have known of the cognitive func-tion of metaphor.

Freud explained the continuity and the displaceability of sexual desire as due to the vicissitudes of psychic energy. What Freud attributed to the vicissitudes of psychic energy can now be attributed to the power of metaphoric transfor-mation.[4] Freud found *libido* difficult to define but thought of it as a form of sexual psychic energy. He did not think of psychic energy as a scientific metaphor, for he felt that he was describing a physical actuality. (At the end of the nineteenth and beginning of the twentieth centuries it was commonplace for biologists to invoke the concept of energy, as in Newtonian physics, if they wished to be differentiated from vitalists.) Freud was well aware of the transformations of libido, but he insisted on retaining the idea of libido as a kind of Platonic entity.

One singular aspect of our emotions that I believe to be uniquely human is that feelings derived from different bio-logical systems can be substituted for each other. In his *Three Essays on the Theory of Sexuality* (1905), Freud alludes to the process whereby an instinctual system serving one function can be transferred onto another system, serving a very dif-ferent function (see Modell 1997). Freud was attempting to explain the obvious fact that sucking acquired a sex-ual meaning. Freud said, "To begin with, sexual activity attaches itself to functions serving the purpose of self-preservation [nursing] and does not become independent of them until later" (1905). And further: "At a time at which the first beginnings of sexual satisfaction are still linked with the taking of nourishment, the sexual instinct has a sexual object outside the infant's own body in the shape of his mother's breast" (1905).

Although nursing and maternal attachment and sexuality are separate biological systems, the emotions and feelings associated with these systems are conflated, by means of an unconscious metaphoric process. Other familiar examples of libidinal conflation, displacements, and transformations are the eroticization of anxiety and the eroticization of shame and humiliation. These transformations of feeling may be enabled by a kind of physiological metonymy (where a part substitutes for the whole). For example, a rapid heart rate is common to both anxiety and sexual arousal, and facial flushing characterizes both shame and sexual arousal.

Conflating Feelings

The eroticization of feelings of humiliation is a familiar example of the conflation of very different affect systems, which, as I have noted, is a uniquely human attribute. The conflation of feelings of humiliation and erotic excitement can be illustrated by the narrative structure of certain fantasies. These accounts also illustrate the importance of unconscious intentionality as a director of the corporeal imagination. The conflation of erotic feelings and humiliation is evident in fantasies of being beaten.[5] I have no way of estimating the prevalence of fantasies of being beaten, but the writer Daphne Merkin, in a *New Yorker* article (1996), described her life-long preoccupation with fantasies of being beaten on the buttocks. Fantasies of being beaten, controlled, and humiliated may, for some, be necessary to achieve orgasm. A humiliating fantasy of this sort may take the following form: *one is taken captive by a man (or woman) and is humiliated by being forced to urinate or defecate in front of the other.* It is well recognized in our culture that losing control of one's bladder or rectum is the source of intense shame and humiliation. But the release of a pent-up substance can also serve as a perceptual metaphor for orgasm. Metaphor unites these seemingly disparate feelings because they share this similarity: a spreading sensation of fullness, followed by release. When the scene in which one is forced by the other to urinate and defecate accompanies the act of sexual intercourse, there is a conflation in fantasy of the bodily functions of urination, defecation, and genital orgasm. Within the fantasy there is also a play of similarity and difference among urination, defecation, and genital orgasm. There is both a fusion and a confusion of functions that can be controlled by the self, such as urination and defecation, and a function that cannot be fully controlled, sexual orgasm. Not uncommonly, such fantasies of being controlled by another occur in individuals who fear loss of control but also wish to avoid responsibility for their sexual feelings. They retain control by means of the fantasy, yet at the same time, within the fantasy, responsibility for sexual arousal is attributed to someone else. As the individual always knows that he or she is the author of the fantasy, a sense of autonomy is nevertheless preserved. But there is a paradox—for although one is in control of the fantasy, the content of the fantasy, limited as it is to humiliating scenes, indicates that the imagination is directed and to some extent involuntary. The structure of the fantasy shares the polysemy, the systematically related multiple meanings, as well as the unconscious intentionality that we observed in Freud's dream of the Botanical Monograph.

Freud's assumption that libido is a universal instinct would lead him to describe this fantasy as perverse (as an infantile regression). Viewed from the perspective of an autonomous imagination, this fantasy contains nothing relevant to the ideas of perversion, fixation, or regression. Inasmuch as the functional intent of the constructed scene is directed towards the present, this fantasy or constructed scene could be described, not as a perversion, but as part of Merleau-Ponty's "intentional arc," directed towards the here and now. "The life of consciousness—cognitive life, the life of desire—is subtended by an 'intentional arc,' which projects round about us our past, our future, our human setting" (Merleau-Ponty 1962, p. 136). I will further explore this unconscious intentionality in the following chapter.

5   Intentionality
       and the Self

An "intent" is the directing of an action toward some future goal that is defined and chosen by the actor.

Thomas Aquinas

Every organism has a world of its own because it has an experience of its own.

Ernst Cassirer

Intentionality is implicitly an ecological concept in that action in the environment alters that environment, and in turn the environment alters the self. Intentionality, whether conscious or unconscious, can be thought of as a value-driven selection directed towards some *future* goal. Intentionality therefore includes *the self, emotions,* and *the anticipation of the future,* a form of imagination.

William James (1890), whose account of the phenomenology of self remains unsurpassed, observed that the body is the innermost core of the self. This central nucleus of the self, what he described as this "palpitating inward life," consists of feelings. Freud also believed that the ego (self) "is first and foremost a bodily ego" (1923a). In 1923 the neuropsychiatrist Paul Schilder published *Körperschema* (schema of the body), which was later incorporated into *The Image and Appearance of the Human Body* (Schilder 1935). There he stated that the schema of the body develops and is maintained within the ever changing alternation and continual interplay of the body and the environment, thus developing an early ecological theory of the self.

As the self is known to be embodied, it was inevitable that the origins of the self would be examined in the context of the evolution of the brain. One would then ask what is the function of the self and how does consciousness of the self enhance the individual's fitness. Among the first to propose an evolutionary theory of the self was Gerald Edelman in *The Remembered Present* (1989). He linked the self to a more evolved and complex consciousness. In Edelman's view, the evolution of a self requires a neural apparatus capable of providing the individual with a schema of past, present, and future. Such a schema would enable internal reflection, a consciousness of consciousness. This in turn would free the individual of the necessity of an immediate response to environmental inputs; it would in effect enable one to go offline. Such a self-reflective capacity requires what Edelman called "higher-order consciousness," in contrast to primary consciousness, which we share with many other species. Primary consciousness creates an immediate scene, in which long-term affect-laden memory is salient. In addition, it is assumed that conscious animals can differentiate self from nonself, but this capacity is not to be confused with a sense of personhood. Edelman suggested that there are specific neural structures that enable this self/nonself distinction. He wrote, "Self is fundamentally determined by the signaling activity of areas mediating homeostatic—autonomic, hedonic, neuroendocrine—brain functions. Such areas include brain stem and pontine nuclei, mesencephalic reticular formation, hypothalamus, amygdala, septum and fornix, and their various connections to prelimbic forebrain areas. In contrast, nonself signals are composed of cortico-thalamic inputs and of cerebellar and hippocampal loops other than those in the fornical path" (Edelman 1989, p. 98).

But, as I noted, the biological self that can differentiate self from nonself, which we share with other species, is by no means the same as the self-reflective self that we equate with a sense of personhood.

The Embodied Self as a Monitor of Affective States

Jaak Panksepp (1998a, 1998b), a psychobiologist who has devoted his career to the investigation of the neural corre-lates of emotion, has described a biological *protoself* that functions unconsciously and is of very ancient evolutionary origin. Panksepp believes that the neural correlates of the protoself are associated principally with one of the struc-tures that Edelman has cited—the mesencephalic reticular formation. More specifically, Panksepp refers to an area identified as periaqueductal gray (PAG), which he believes is the site of origin of several basic emotional systems. This area of the midbrain is further characterized anatomically by the diffuseness and the extensiveness of its synaptic con-nections and the presence of cells that produce neuromodu-lators, such as dopamine and serotonin, that orchestrate global reactions in the individual (Nauta and Feirtag 1986). This area functions as a primitive center of homeostasis.

Panksepp suggests that this archaic mesencephalic area monitors the organism's *holistic* affective state and in this sense serves as a progenitor of a sense of self.[1] This unconscious protoself is thought by Panksepp to be an internal point of reference that responds to and compares changes in the organism's affective states. Inasmuch as the midbrain made its appearance in the earliest vertebrates (Allman 1999), it seems highly probable that unconscious monitoring of the organism's holistic affective state occurred before the evolution of consciousness. We must then assume that emotions provided vital information to the individual animal without the need for consciousness. No one knows when consciousness made its appearance. Some believe that all vertebrates may have some form of consciousness. I believe that at least all mammals are conscious and would also attribute consciousness to intelligent birds, such as grey parrots. But it is reasonable to assume that those species lacking consciousness would unconsciously respond to changes in their emotional state. Parenthetically, this would provide a biological backing for the psychoanalyst's unquestioned belief in the existence of unconscious affects. For we share with other species an ancient midbrain.[2] When an animal is endowed with consciousness, this unconscious protoself would then inform an unconscious affective core, the nucleus of a biological self. The term *self* is appropriate in that the biological *self* refers to state functions representative of the entire organism.

This unconscious affective core, to which consciousness has access, contributes not only to an awareness of self and other but also to a sense of the continuity of the self. If animals could speak, they would say, "I know that I am who I am." This concept of self as the monitor of the individual's holistic state has been elaborated by Antonio Damasio (1999) and described as the conscious "core" self,[3] which in turn rests upon Panksepp's unconscious protoself.

Can Consciousness Be Equated with Consciousness of the Self?

Antonio Damasio, in *The Feeling of What Happens* (1999), believes that consciousness cannot be differentiated from consciousness of self, because consciousness is always imbued with feelings and feelings are implicitly an awareness of self. Damasio differentiates conscious *feeling* from unconscious *emotion*. This is a convention that has been implicit in psychoanalytic thought and one that I fully endorse and have adopted. (The differentiation of emotion and feeling will be discussed in greater detail in chapters 7 and 8.) Consciousness may be equated with a feeling state, but how does a feeling state define a self?

Damasio makes the valid observation that we attribute consciousness to dogs because we know that they have feelings and we also know that dogs are aware of and respond to our feelings. Darwin (1872) had no doubt about this matter: he knew that dogs love and wish to be loved. If our dogs acted like zombies, we would doubt that they were conscious.

The biological self that monitors feelings is not the same as a "higher-order" self that is equated with self-awareness and provides a sense of personhood. Awareness of feelings is not the same as a reflective self-awareness, or the awareness of self in relation to others, what William James called the social self. Conscious animals are by definition aware of their feelings, but very few species have what can be called a social self. What, then, is the relation between the biological self, consciousness, and the social self?

Self-awareness, recognition of oneself as a unique person, implies both self-reflection and consciousness of self in a social context. Social animals, such as bonobos and chimpanzees, do have a sense of self-awareness that may represent an adaptation to the requirements of their complex social relationships. Although chimpanzees and bonobos do have a sense of self-awareness, whether or not they have a sense of awareness of other minds is controversial.[4] (I will discuss the awareness of other minds in chapter 9.) Sue Savage-Rumbaugh and Roger Lewin (1994) describe a classic experiment to determine whether chimpanzees are able to recognize their own images in a mirror. A red dot was placed on their foreheads while they were anesthetized. The chimpanzees paid no attention to the dot until they happened to glance in the mirror. Then they noticed the dot and immediately set about removing it. These authors were able to confirm this classic experiment by observing that their six-month-old chimpanzee Panzi nicked her browridge enough that a tiny red scrape appeared. Panzi happened to be walking by the mirror and as usual stopped to glance at her reflection. This time, however, she paused, sat down, and gazed intently for about 45 seconds. Then she slowly reached up to touch the red spot on her forehead with her index finger while watching herself in the mirror. After touching the spot, she then looked at her finger, but there was no blood, as the scrape was so slight.

Panzi's capacity for self-recognition in the mirror at six months of age is precocious when compared to a human infant. For such mirror recognition does not appear in human infants until 18 months (Emde 1983).[5]

As might be expected, awareness of the self / other distinction appears much earlier in human infants than awareness of the self as a social entity. Daniel Stern (1985) reports that Siamese twins who sucked each other's fingers were able to differentiate their own hands from those of the other. Stern describes an early core self in which the infant is aware that it is the agent of action. This sense of agency is an aspect of the "core self" that is present in early infancy and persists throughout our lives. This sense of agency, when present, contributes to a sense of joyful well-being.

We should note the significance of Panksepp's observation that the midbrain affective neural structures anatomically converge to provide the individual with an unconscious monitoring of their global affective states. This protoself is the source of *a point of reference* that describes the individual's overall state. This unconscious biological self presages the fact that awareness of self in a social context, the social self,[6] will also function as an internal monitor of one's overall state. This unconscious monitoring of the individual's global affective state contributes to the individual's sense of the uniqueness and coherence and continuity of the self. In *The Private Self* (Modell 1993) I recognized that the need to maintain the continuity and coherence of the self is a vital function that is of no less importance than sexuality or attachment to others. I suggested that the continuity and coherence of the self can be thought of as a psychobiological "homeostat" (Modell 1993). Damasio (1999) proposes something similar in his concept of the core self. However, consciousness is not necessarily coterminous with the social self.

For example, consider the situation when I'm driving to the grocery store and, since I do not like writing lists, I am rehearsing in my mind what I need to purchase and at the same time I am also conscious of my driving and the visual scene ahead of me. In the scene that I am describing, a reflective consciousness of self in a social context is not in evidence. However, let us imagine that, in the course of this journey to the grocery store, I remember that a recent article in a professional journal ignored what I justly thought to be my own contribution to the subject in question. I might then feel humiliation, a point of reference and comparison to others, and feel a depletion of the self. At this juncture I am conscious of my personhood and a social self.

Such holistic referencing may originate in the biological self as a monitor of feeling, and in the course of development, such referencing becomes part of self-reflection. It hardly needs to be added that self-reflection is an imaginative function that can be directed by conscious and unconscious fantasy (as I shall discuss later in this chapter and in chapter 6) and forms no part of the biological self. The unity of consciousness may be experienced as a sense of self, but as I have illustrated, consciousness contains many windows and does not always contain the window of self-reflection.

An Ecological Approach to the Self's Construction of Meaning

Walter Freeman's (1999a, 1999b) expansion of the concept of intentionality unites and synthesizes what many in cognitive science view as separate faculties: imagination, memory, motivation, and perception. This concept of intentionality is also consistent with everything that I know from my experience as a psychoanalyst. Let me review what I presented earlier in chapter 1. Freeman proposed that "meanings arise as a brain creates intentional behaviors and then changes itself in accordance with the sensory consequences of those behaviors." To avoid the errors implicit in Descartes' concept of mental representation, Freeman embraced the idea of intentionality as described by Thomas Aquinas in 1264. Thomas Aquinas denoted as intentionality the process by which humans and other animals act in accordance with their own growth and maturation. An *intent* is the directing of action toward some future goal *defined and chosen by the actor.* Perception is a selective action that may be unconscious. Intentionality, as redefined and expanded by Freeman, is the means by which the organism creates meaning by action in the environment and assimilating that action into the self.

Intentionality as redefined in this manner is quite different from the term as used by Brentano and other philosophers, such as Searle (1983), in that it avoids the problems of representation and correspondence of meaning. Intentionality as redefined is not about "aboutness." Meaning is achieved through *action* in the world, and in turn, the self is altered by that action. This is a point of view that is shared by pragmatic philosophers such as John Dewey and is consistent with an ecological approach to perception proposed by Piaget (1954), James Gibson (1986), and Andy Clark (1997). Freeman's intentionality is similar to Merleau-Ponty's "intentional arc," where the self repeats cycles of action and perception in order to obtain "maximum grip."

An ecological analogy is therefore implicit when we think of the self in relation to its human and inanimate environment. The self creates its own ecological niche, for every individual lives within their own *Umwelt,* which is created from within as well as provided from without. The term *Umwelt* was popularized by Jakob Von Uexkull in 1934. He defined it as "those environmental features to which a given animal is sensitized, so that each species constructs their own perceptual world" (cited in Clark 1997). Von Uexkull described the behavior of the tick that is sensitive to the butyric acid present on the skin of mammals. When this acid is detected, the tick relinquishes its hold on the object that it is clinging to and then drops on the animal. The tick's perceptual world is dominated by butyric acid; the tick's nervous system has selection barriers to prevent the transfer of unwanted information from the environment. To state the matter differently, the detection of butyric acid is a transcendent value for the tick.

Unconscious Intentionality in an Intersubjective Context

We assume that the tick's sensitivity to butyric acid is determined by its genetic code and becomes expressed as a value-driven selection. Our own intentionality is also subject to value-driven selection that can be directly attributed not to our genes but to our unconscious memory and desires. Value-driven selection will determine what information we will assimilate and what we will exclude from our inner world and from our perception of others in our human environment.

Let us consider the following clinical fragment: A woman's loving relationship with her father was irrevocably lost when, in her early childhood, her father developed a brain tumor that led to the gradual deterioration of his personality and his eventual death. As an adult, she was compulsively driven to uncover defects in men, almost is if it were a matter of her survival. These presumed defects were then selectively perceived to the exclusion of whatever other virtues might be present. For example, she noted that her husband was driving slowly, overly cautiously, and, in her judgment, incompetently. She then wondered whether he was developing brain damage and becoming precociously senile. She became enraged at him and afterwards guilty because of the irrationality of her reaction. The intensity of her rage frightened her. She thought that she was going a bit crazy, as if she had momentarily fallen into a time warp, for driving with her husband recreated in her imagination a similar scene from her childhood when she was a five-year-old little girl sitting next to her father in the family car. As a result of his illness, her father was visually impaired and could barely see the road, and she was terrified that they would be killed.

Let us now attempt to deconstruct her response and examine the various determinants of motivation, memory, and perception that lie behind this example of unconscious intentionality. You will recall that all memory, including emotional memory, is nonrepresentational—that the activation of memory is not analogous to retrieving items from a storage bank, items that replicate previous events. Instead, emotional memory exists as a *potential* that is activated by elements within the context of present experience. In this process of retrieval, metaphor *is the interpreter of unconscious memory,* and metonymy directs perception. The past predicts the future.

During the process of retrieval, potential memorial categories become activated as a result of their metaphoric similarity. In the preceding illustration, a potential affect category, an emotional constellation that serves as an organizer for memory, can be described as the terror that ensues when she seeks care and protection from someone whom she perceives as incompetent. To be dependent on someone who is incompetent threatens her sense of safety in the world.

In this instance unconscious intentionality both selects and deselects perceptual items. This process is activated by metonymic association, in this example, by the woman's perception of her husband's overly cautious driving, which then triggered an entire scene from childhood with all its accompanying feelings. The metaphoric matching between her emotionally charged memories of the past and her current experience was then felt to be an exact fit. She experienced only a sense of similarity and not a sense of difference. This can be described as an illustration of involuntary imagination in which the memory of an entire ensemble of feelings from the past is substituted for present experience. She constructed a scene that changed her world. In this process, metonymy and metaphor played a crucial role. For this reason I will examine metonymy itself, for its role in unconscious intentionality should not be underestimated.

Metonymy as an Affective Marker

If salient unconscious memories exist as potentials for actions in the world, present metonymic associations activate such unconscious memories. Metonymy, like metaphor, is primarily an element of cognition and thought and is not simply a trope or a figure of speech. Like metaphor, metonymy pervades our thinking and consequently our speech. Metonymy is defined as a substitution of the part for the whole. A classic example was provided by Lakoff: one waitress says to another, "The ham sandwich just spilled beer all over himself" (1987).

Linguists and philosophers have debated whether metonymy is different from, or similar to, metaphor (Gibbs 1993). My clinical examples would indicate that metaphor and metonymy are indeed different but operate synergistically. In human relationships, one may react to an isolated element that one perceives in another person, the part signifying the whole. This metonymic association might then evoke an intense affective experience because of a metaphoric match of the present with a corresponding unconscious memory. This can be described as a transference of everyday life. *The feelings that were once meaningful in the context of the past are felt to be irrational in the context of the present.*[7]

Although it appears from the foregoing illustration that metaphor and metonymy operate synergistically, the eminent linguist Roman Jakobson (1995), as I noted in the previous chapter, viewed metonymy and metaphor as competitive rather than synergistic. He said, "A competition between both devices, metonymic and metaphoric, is manifest in any symbolic process, be it interpersonal or social" (Jakobson 1995, p. 132). He believed that metaphor and metonymy are binomial elements encoded in the structure of language. Sir James Frazer's *The Golden Bough* (1994) influenced Jakobson's analysis of magical thought. Frazer (1994, p. 105) categorized magic into two divisions: one sympathetic, that is, imitative or homeopathic, and the other as contagious. Homeopathic magic is based on the idea of similarity, that like produces like, that like things act upon each other at a distance through a secret sympathy. Contagious magic, on the other hand, is based on the thought that things once having been in contact with each other are always in contact with each other. It is then a short step to believe that in this contact a part can substitute for the whole. Jakobson postulated that sympathetic magic is based on metaphor (homeopathy), and contagious magic on metonymy.

Metonymy and contagious magic are still very much part of our belief systems in that we experience a pleasurable expansion of the self when we figuratively touch or are touched by the great and famous. This is the obvious function of name-dropping, where we enjoy the effects of positive contagious magic. Negative contagion has its expression in our avoidance of losers and our avoidance of the sick and dying.

Unconscious Intentionality in a Neural Context

The neuroscientist Benjamin Libet (1999) has demonstrated experimentally that our willing something to happen, our conscious intent, is preceded by an unconscious neural event. This neural event may be described as the correlate of unconscious intentionality. Libet discovered that brain activity, what he called a "readiness potential," preceded a subject's conscious intention by approximately 0.5 seconds. The experimental subjects were asked to flex their wrists. They were also provided with a timing device that enabled them to record within a fraction of a second when they were aware of their conscious intention to move their wrists. When asked to spontaneously flex their wrists, unconscious brain activation occurred approximately one-half second before they were conscious of their intent. I believe that it was significant that the subjects knew something of the nature of the task beforehand, that expectancy was part of the experimental setup, which may have then "primed" their unconscious.

This experimental demonstration of cortical activation occurring before conscious intent raises the problem of free will. Are we our brain's master? Are our conscious intents truly voluntary? To what extent did an unconscious readiness potential influence the subjects intent to act? Is our belief in conscious intentionality, that the self initiates action, that we are independent actors, an illusion? Libet (1999) maintains that his experiments did not decide the question of free will. Although in this experiment the time interval between the readiness potential of the subject's conscious intent was of short duration and invariant, his research has obvious implications for the broader issue of unconscious intentionality outside of an experimental setup, where the

relation between unconscious intent and conscious awareness of that intent is more unpredictable. In addition to
speaking to the problem of free will, Libet's work is important also in that *he has scientifically demonstrated that unconscious intentionality occurs in the waking state.*

Unconscious intentionality may activate an unconscious
metaphoric process such as occurs in dreaming and creative
thinking, as described in chapter 2. Llinás (2001) sees an
analogy between consciousness and dreaming in that both
are self-generated, bootstrapping processes that provide a
ready-made context for sensory inputs. Therefore, the analogy of consciousness to the dream state is apt, for dreaming
illustrates the brain's intrinsic activity when it is relatively
cut off from incoming stimulation.

Some dreams may be generated by a problem or task that
directs one's thoughts and creates a sense of expectancy. As
Merleau-Ponty observed, "During the dream we do not
leave the world behind; the world obsesses us even during
sleep" (1962, p. 293). The unconscious requires priming;
there must be a *desire* to find a solution. It is evident that
while we are awake, the unconscious is attuned and activated to the expectations and immediate demands of life as
it is lived.

A Self-Created *Umwelt*

Psychoanalysts assume that an unconscious intentionality
operates intersubjectively, that is, that we are influenced
by our unconscious intentionality and we may also perceive the other's unconscious intentionality. Unconsciously
aroused feeling states may characterize all intimate relationships and are especially evident in the relationship between
patient and analyst. Such feeling states can become so

pervasive as to become an environmental surround. This
ambience of feeling that surrounds us is analogous to our
inanimate environment, but it is an environment that we
create for ourselves as a set of *expectations*. We know that
the quality of the air we breathe and the level of the noise
we hear affects us. I would claim that the emotional ambience that we create in relation to others can be thought of
as a human environment that affects us as profoundly as
does our inanimate environment.

This analogy forms a part of the ecological metaphor that
the self creates its own ecological niche, that every individual lives within their own *Umwelt*, which is created from
within as well as provided from without—a process in
which unconscious intentionality plays a salient role. I can
illustrate this by means of a hypothetical example. Let us
consider an individual who is fearful and distrustful of others. Let us further imagine that he will selectively perceive
only the hostile intent in the other person and deselect and
close off any perception of positive feeling. Accordingly, his
hostile unconscious intent is communicated to and will be
perceived by the other person. This will evoke a correspondingly negative reaction in the other, which the subject will
then experience as a confirmation of his original distrust.
Our subject has created an environment of anger and distrust. We can conclude that his unconscious intentionality
has created an environment derived from his own imagination. The subject's intentional act has made the boundary
between self and other more permeable. In this sense, the
environment is not fixed but can be molded by the subject.
The self has entered into a human environment and is altered by what it perceives. But what it perceives is also a
creation of the self. This illustration is an example of creating
an imaginary "other," but the involuntary and compulsive

nature of the process indicates a constriction of the imagination that keeps it from creating new meaning.

Images and Imagination

This section, which describes the relation between imagination and intentionality, is intended to serve as an introduction to the chapter that follows. Let as assume *that the synthetic function of imagination is uniquely human, but that imaging is a widespread function that we share with other species.* We should therefore distinguish between imaging and imagination.[8] Imagination is unquestionably an aspect of intentionality. Perception, memory, and imagination are all interwoven into the fabric of intentionality and will determine the nature of our actions in the world. Acknowledging the role of imagination in intentionality makes it impossible to view imagination and perception as separate faculties. It is therefore misleading to contrast imagination with reality. Freud may have contributed to this misunderstanding when he linked fantasy to the pleasure principle. He wrote, "With the introduction of the reality principle, one species of thought-activity was split off; it was kept free from reality testing and remained subject to the pleasure principle alone. This activity is 'phantasying'" (Freud 1911, p. 222).[9]

Cornelius Castoriadis (1922–1997) has provided us with an elegant account of Aristotle's concept of imagination (1987; 1997, p. 194). Castoriadis, perhaps more than any other contemporary philosopher, has recognized the centrality of imagination. He sees imagination as a defining element in our humanity and a determining element in our social institutions (Castoriadis 1987, 1997). I will repeat his words that serve as the introductory epigraph to this book: "What is most human is not rationalism but the uncontrolled and incontrollable continuous surge of creative radical imagination."

Castoriadis recognized the contemporary relevance of Aristotle's view that imagination and intentionality are inseparable. Aristotle (1986), who defined imagination as a "sensation without matter," said, "The soul never thinks without phantasm" and "There's no desiring without imagination." Thought always involves a reference to things not present to the senses (but present to the imagination). To paraphrase Aristotle, thoughts always contain unseen comparisons to what can be only imagined. Aristotle was absolutely correct in believing that thinking is not possible without imagination.[10]

Imagination mobilizes images, but a moment's reflection will tell us that there is a difference between images generated from remembered perceptions and images generated from feelings within our body, images that become images of desire. Images of the former type have been the province of academic psychology, while images of the latter type have been of special interest to psychoanalysts.

How, then, are the images of desire generated? How are erotic feelings transformed into images? This is, of course, the crux of the so-called mind/body problem. It is the problem of explaining the emergence of consciousness from unconscious neural processes, the emergence of a feeling self from an unconscious protoself. Castoriadis (1987, 1997) has dealt at length with Freud's answer to this problem. To recall what I noted in chapter 3, Freud did not recognize an autonomous imagination. Instead of imagination, Freud spoke of fantasy. Fantasy, Freud believed, is a *representation* of an instinct or drive. Freud explained the transformation of an unconscious somatic process into a mental image by means of this political metaphor of *representation*. The

English term *representation* is a translation of the German *Repräsentanz*, "a delegation, a mission, representing a government, or constituted body" (Castoriadis 1997). If fantasy is understood to be a *representation* of instinct, Freud was saying that the process of transforming an instinctual urge into a fantasy can be thought of as a delegation between two separate governing bodies, with the implication that they can arrive at some common language.

The images derived from perception and memory may pale in some individuals when compared to the images derived from feelings of lust, anxiety, or rage. There is probably a significant degree of individual difference.[11] When William James addressed the subject of imagination in his *Principles of Psychology* (1890), he focused almost exclusively on visual imagery. He summarized the research that was available to him at that time and emphasized the *striking degree of individual differences* in the capacity to form visual images (an argument for the autonomy of the imagination). James wondered about the brain's activity in forming such images and suggested that sensation and imagination utilize the same areas in the cerebral cortex. Approximately one hundred years later this speculation appears to be confirmed by Stephen Kosslyn and his colleagues (Kosslyn, Pacual-Leone, et al. 1999). Their subjects were asked to memorize a visual display consisting of stripes of various sizes placed in different quadrants of a scaled graph. With their eyes shut, they were asked to judge the dimension of the stripes in the different quadrants. Simultaneously, their brains were scanned using PET. It was observed that an area of the visual cortex (area 17) was activated. Although these findings await further confirmation, it seems likely that vision and visual imagination utilize similar neural circuitry.

Earlier I have also referred to Panksepp's (1998a, 1998b) concept of a protoself that monitors emotions and impulses generated in the midbrain. Emotions include not only lust, for Panksepp identifies the following affect centers in the midbrain: fear, rage, lust, and attachment seeking. Some of these affects can be categorized as pleasurable, but it is significant that pain has no representation. The aesthetician Elaine Scarry, in *The Body in Pain* (1985), makes the important observation that pain, unlike desires, does not have a point of reference, a corresponding object in the external world. She writes, "The man 'desiring' can see the rain and note that it is its cessation that he is longing for, so that he can go out and find berries he is hungry for, before of the night comes that he fears. Because of the inevitable bonding of his own interior states with companion objects in the outside world, he easily locates himself in the external world and has no need to invent the world to extend himself out into. The object is an extension of, an expression of, the state: the rain expresses his longing, the berries his hunger, and the night his fear. But nothing expresses his physical pain" (1985, p. 162).

Pain does not resonate with the external world. We can imagine and anticipate (physical) pain, but when we actually experience pain, the sensation itself does not generate images or metaphors as desires generate images. This, of course, does not negate the fact that mental pain can be metaphorically used in the service of other needs and desires, as exemplified by sadomasochism. We are all familiar with the observation that physical pain may be used as the metaphoric substitute for psychological pain.

6   Directing the Imagination

Consciousness itself will furnish proofs by its own direction that it is connected with master-currents below the surface.

Samuel Taylor Coleridge

Although one's imagination is autonomous, it can also be directed to a degree that excludes the agency of the self, as in cases of trauma, where feelings and thoughts are stereotypic and constricted in ways analogous to a fixed-action pattern. One's imagination is therefore subject to varying degrees of freedom. Imagination can be constricted by trauma or expanded through empathy and aesthetic experience. This chapter will examine these forces that expand or constrict the imagination.

Images and Homeostasis

Although we cannot know the content of an animal's mind, if one thinks of Pavlov's dogs, conditioned to salivate at the sound of a bell, it seems likely that the conditioned reflex, the bell, evokes an image of food. Expectancy, an aspect of intentionality, refers to the immediate future, and the future can only be imagined.

Animals do not require language to recognize an image. Animals need to remember where food is hidden and the location of a watering hole. It seems probable that such intentionality is prompted by visual images. If this is true, it would support the assumption that consciousness is more widespread.

When one's vital interests are at stake, the evocation of involuntary images likely serves an adaptive function. This suggests that the evocation of snapshot images is a primitive mental function that is not uniquely human. It is probable, as I have suggested, that such images are used in the service of homeostasis. For example, elephants in times of drought desperately need to find watering holes, and it is reasonable to suppose that this search would be facilitated by images of remembered watering holes. When a monkey hears the call of a leopard, it is probable that the animal experiences, as an association, an involuntary image of a leopard. We know that alarm calls in vervet monkeys carry semantic information. These monkeys produce distinctive alarm calls in response to three different classes of predators: big cats, birds of prey, and snakes (Hauser 2000). Their alarm signals communicate not only emotions but also specific vital information that will prompt the very different escape strategies that the monkeys must employ to avoid being eaten. Again, it is a reasonable hypothesis that each of these differentiated alarm calls will evoke a specific visual image of a predator, an image of a leopard, an eagle, or a snake.

The Involuntary Imagination of Trauma

The metonymic associations of the memory of trauma may be homologous to the automatic imagery that the animal experiences when vital needs are at stake. The degree of freedom of the imagination is limited. When metonymic associations of trauma arouse the imagination, danger is anticipated. An involuntary scene is created in which images from the past dominate and suffuse current perceptions.

You will recall the example of the man who panicked when he was unable to return home because of an airline strike. Metonymic associations activated a forgotten affect category—a scene from childhood where his family was helpless and their lives endangered in the face of Nazi intransigence. The imagined scene, created from memories from the age of three, was transposed to the present, and the result was an overwhelming panic. In another example, a woman became enraged in response to her husband's slow and inept driving. This partial and highly selected perception was associatively linked through metonymy to her seriously impaired father. The present scene was transformed in her imagination into one where her damaged father, and not her husband, was driving the car, and she felt her life to be endangered. The imaginary images created in response to the metonymic associations of the memory of trauma are like images created in other species as a response to life-threatening situations.

In these examples the imaginative process is automatic, involuntary, and foreclosed, as if it were a fixed-action pattern. A selective interpretation does not contribute to the imaginative process. The metaphoric correspondence between past and present is frozen and inflexible, and consciousness loses a measure of complexity as it is limited to a single gestalt. This loss of the creative, synthetic function of metaphor is a characteristic response to trauma, and it threatens the integrity of the self. Trauma degrades metaphor, and massive trauma degrades metaphor absolutely. Holocaust survivors reported later that during the time of the holocaust they lived in a world that is beyond metaphor (Bergmann and Jucovy 1982, Grubrich-Simitis 1984).

The Aesthetic Imagination and the Brain

Elaine Scarry (1999) has attempted to explain the seemingly mysterious methods that a poet or novelist employs that directs the reader to construct a visual scene from only printed words. How does the written word evoke a vibrant visual image? Her answer is that novelists and poets from the time of Homer to the present have, by means of words, *imitated how the brain perceives images.* This imitation of the brain's own perceptual process expands the reader's visual imagination. The author, by imitating the visual process that occurs in the brain, *directs* the reader's imagination. I shall not attempt to reproduce here her complex discussion, but a simplified version would be that descriptions of motion, overlapping surfaces, and especially descriptions of color activate our visual imagination.[1] Scarry believes that a description of flowers is especially important in enabling the reader to visualize scenes. It would appear that color is salient. However, Scarry attributes to flowers a much more complex and specific role, which may represent her own particular way of forming images. There is an implied priming of the visual scene in that easily visualized images, such as flowers or circular motion, will spread to less easily visualized items. She would claim that major literary artists intuitively know how the brain creates images.

Scarry's thesis was given some support by a PET study that demonstrated that reading words denoting color will stimulate regions of the temporal cortex adjacent to those involved in the perception of color, and reading words denoting action will stimulate areas in the temporal cortex that register the perception of motion (Martin, Haxby, et al. 1995). This study is consistent with the contention that imagination imitates perception both experientially and neurologically.

Semir Zeki, an eminent investigator of the neurophysiology of vision, has independently arrived at a similar view with regard to visual art. He said, "The aims of art constitute an extension of the functions of the brain" (Zeki 1999). He believes that artists expand the visual imagination by intensifying the excitation of specific areas in the visual brain. It is now well established that our visual cortex consists of modular elements in that there are specialized clusters of cells for the detection of color, the direction and velocity of motion, and the orientation of lines, whether vertical or horizontal. Although the difference is only a matter of milliseconds, there is a temporal sequence or temporal hierarchy to visual perception in that color is perceived before form, which is perceived before motion (Zeki 1999). This might explain Scarry's proposal that the greatest novelists and poets (Homer, Flaubert, Rilke) describe flowers, contrasting forms, and motion in order to awaken and enlarge the reader's visual imagination. But it is evident that literature excites more than the visual imagination; it excites our empathic imagination, our capacity to vicariously experience the world as seen through the minds of others.

What Scarry found to be true of literature, Zeki found to be true of painting and sculpture. Zeki (1999) believes that major artists intensify the imagination by intuitively or unintentionally imitating the manner in which the visual cortex constructs images. You may recall that I referred in chapter 3 to Zeki's description of color vision. Our experience of color as a constant quality is an illusion produced in the visual cortex. The constancy of our subjective experience of color results from a comparison that occurs within the brain. The brain compares the wavelength composition of light reflected from a surface and the wavelength composition of light reflected from surrounding surfaces. The visual cortex constructs the quality of a color by detecting the constant ratio of wavelengths of light reflected from a surface as compared to that of surrounding surfaces (Zeki 1993). Because illumination is continually changing, and because our eyes, heads, and bodies are constantly in motion, objects are continually seen from different perspectives. Therefore, visual constancy is a property of our brain and not of the physical world.

Zeki proposed that the illusion of constancy is also a significant property of visual art. He used Vermeer as an example of an artist who produced an uncanny sense of stillness and constancy in his interiors and at the same time introduced a measure of ambiguity in that one never quite knows what sort of relationship is going on between the people that he depicted.[2]

I would agree with Zeki that constancy, when combined with ambiguity, excites and expands the imagination. In a very different context I have suggested something similar regarding an analogy between play and the psychoanalytic process. In *Other Times, Other Realities* (Modell 1990), I observed that play is fundamentally paradoxical in that the essence of play is its freedom and spontaneity but it is a freedom that must occur within a certain constancy, a constancy due to the rules of the game. The psychoanalytic situation is similar to play in that there is a constancy and regularity with regard to time and the physical setup but there is a built-in ambiguity regarding the emotional relationship, as in a Vermeer painting. The psychoanalytic setup is intended to expand the imagination.

In view of the modularity of the visual cortex, Zeki maintains that some artists discovered that they could obtain special effects by exciting specific areas of the visual cortex. An example would be Mondrian's use of lines and rectangles. Those artists who imitate motion in paintings and sculpture, so-called kinetic art, excite a different area of the visual brain, V5. Zeki believes that the hyperstimulation of selected areas of the visual cortex when viewing an ambiguous painting or sculpture expands the viewer's imagination. In the examples provided by Scarry and Zeki, the artist gently directs the reader's or viewer's imagination by means of a medium that is sufficiently unclear that the self is invited to enter into the construction of the image. Zeki suspects that this is the reason that Michelangelo intentionally created ambiguity when he left several of his sculptures unfinished.

The Empathic Imagination

The critic and novelist Cynthia Ozick tells us, "Metaphor relies on what has been experienced before and therefore transforms the strange into the familiar. Without metaphor we cannot imagine what it is to be someone else, we cannot imagine the life of the Other" (1991).

The extent to which the self can enter into the other can be seen as an expression of the freedom of the imagination. In imagining the other person, the self is constrained by its own vital needs, and the degree to which it is constrained will in turn limit the complexity that characterizes the image of the other. I can illustrate this by referring to the empathic imagination and contrasting empathy to a phenomenon psychoanalysts have called *projective identification*. (In the discussion that follows I will restrict the term *empathic imagination* to refer only to people, and not to literature or inanimate works of art.) We usually think of empathy as a form of voluntary imagination in which there is a sense of the self as agent. The empathic imagination is usually experienced as a kind of pleasurable bonding with the other. It relies on metaphor, for within an empathic connection with the other there is a play of similarity and difference based on metaphor. Empathy requires this play of similarity and difference: one recognizes a sense of identity with the other while at the same time retaining one's sense of self. If this play of similarity and difference is absent, one may experience a sense of total identification with the other, which in some instances may create anxiety. This absence of metaphoric play of similarity and difference can again be linked to trauma. In individuals and families that have been severely traumatized, metaphor becomes degraded: instead of feeling an empathic connection to a parent, a traumatized individual may feel as if he *is* his parent. This is especially evident in children of Holocaust survivors (Bergmann and Jucovy 1982, Grubrich-Simitis 1984).

The term *empathy* is a late-nineteenth-century word, a translation of the German term *Einfühlung,* introduced by the German psychologist Theodor Lipps to denote the projection of the self into the object of perception. For Lipps, the original objects of empathy were works of art. Yet the idea of the self entering into the object of perception did not originate with Lipps, as it can be traced back to Vico. In Isaiah Berlin's account (1969), Vico believed that we can understand the past because others' experience is sufficiently woven into one's own experience and can be revived by means of imagination. Vico was the first to discover that *meaning is constructed through imaginatively entering into the minds of others.*

Samuel Taylor Coleridge, who had read and admired Vico and was probably influenced by him, described imagination as a coalescence of the subject and the object: "Into the simplest seeming 'datum' a constructing, forming activity from the mind has entered. And the perceiving and the forming are the same. The subject (the self) has gone into what it perceives, and what it perceives is, in this sense, itself. So that the object becomes the subject and the subject the object" (Richards 1969, p. 57). Coleridge is saying, in effect, that we should not take the object as something given to us but as something formed through our imagination.

Coleridge's description of imagination as the self entering into what it perceives comes close to our contemporary understanding of empathy. This transitory loss of distinction between self and other also suggests that the roots of empathy may be found in the mirroring of feeling that occurs between mother and child, which may be accompanied by a temporary sense of merging.

Psychoanalysts also understand empathy as a partial or transitory identification, a process in which the self enters into the other. However, there is an important addition: psychoanalysts have observed that the empathic process can also be involuntary and unconscious. In 1926 Helene Deutsch noted that the analyst's unconscious perception of the patient's feelings became transmuted into an inner experience of the analyst.[3] Empathy leads to a pleasurable sense of affective bonding with the other. If, however, the other person unconsciously manipulates our imagination and we do not sense an identification, this is experienced as unpleasurable, and accordingly we do not label such a feeling as empathic.

It appears that we do not have a word that denotes this total, conscious and unconscious, affective impact that one mind has upon another. As I noted, the term *empathy* usually denotes the pleasurable aspect of entering into the mind of another. However, we are all well aware of the fact that the other's unconscious intentionality may evoke in us a variety of negative feelings, such as anxiety, guilt, or rage. Empathy should include the recognition within oneself of negative feelings toward the other. Empathy may result in a modification of the self as the consequence of knowledge of the other. One's sense of self is impacted and altered in the process of assimilating the feelings of the other. Affective knowledge of the other alters the self, and accordingly the self accommodates itself to what is perceived, very much as in Piaget's (1954) description of the child's construction of external reality.

This view is consistent with biological intentionality. Future intent is communicated to another person by means of emotional signals. Emotions are present whether or not the individual providing the signal is conscious of what they are feeling. From the standpoint of the recipient of the feeling, the individual has unconsciously directed the recipient's imagination. But unlike in the examples provided by Scarry and Zeki, where the imagination is expanded and intensified, when the imagination is directed by the process of projective identification, the result will be a constriction or foreclosure of the imagination, as I shall now describe.

Projective Identification

Psychoanalysts occasionally experience a process called *projective identification,* a peculiar kind of emotional interaction with their patients that is initially both puzzling and disturbing. It is a phenomenon of interest not just to psychoanalysts, as it illustrates that emotions can be communicated unconsciously and that the recipient's response is immediate and involuntary. The recent discovery of "mirror neurons" suggests that the unconscious communication of feeling may be explained by an analogous neural mirroring of emotions. Empathy is an unconscious process in which the individual uses his own body as a template that enables him to "feel" into the other's experience [Gallese 2001]. (I will discuss this further in chapter 10.)

Projective identification is a process whereby the patient unconsciously "places" feelings within the analyst. As a consequence, the patient directs the analyst's imagination so that he assumes an alien role that may correspond to the patient's self and the patient's own internalized objects. This phenomenon was initially described by Melanie Klein and later elaborated by the Argentinean psychoanalyst Heinrich Racker (1968). What is of general interest is that the analyst's imagination can be unconsciously directed by the patient with the result that the analyst reexperiences the *same feelings* as did the patient during critical interactions with salient figures from his past. When this occurs, old traumatic relationships that have been internalized by the patient as affective memory are recreated in the present, often with a reversal of roles. As a consequence of this aspect of the patient's unconscious intentionality, the analyst identifies with the patient's projection and discovers that he is assuming a role that may be disturbingly alien to his own sense of self. It is as if the patient has unconsciously acquired the function of a stage director and has assigned a character part to the analyst that the analyst does not want to play.

In my book *Other Times, Other Realities* (1990), I described the following sequence of events. A patient complained that I was not being helpful, as I was not making useful comments or interpretations. I, in turn, was feeling frustrated because I felt that in her withdrawn, mostly silent, unengaged state it was not possible to say anything meaningful or useful. I said (with a slight edge of irritation in my voice), "You want me to produce something out of the blue." To my surprise, this phrase "out of the blue" evoked an intense reaction of rage. I felt dismayed by my patient's explosive rage and moreover felt unjustly attacked. My experience was one of being battered for trying to be helpful and making an "innocent" remark. The attack itself was totally unexpected and felt as if it came "out of the blue." I recalled the cynical aphorism "One's good deeds never go unpunished," and I was also unpleasantly aware that I was feeling sorry for myself.

As a child, this woman experienced her father's intense uncontrolled rage reactions, which could be directed at her for reasons that she could never fathom. The rage appeared out of the blue; she felt herself, as I did, to be an innocent victim, so that my feeling state in my present moment of consciousness corresponded to a feeling state from the patient's past. My irritated tone of voice that accompanied my saying that she wanted me to produce something out of the blue undoubtedly served as a metonymic association of her father's anger. What is of interest in this example of projective identification is that this patient's unconscious intentionality induced in me a replica of her own experiences as a child, and as a consequence I knew how this woman felt when she was the victim of her father's rage. I felt the sense of being unjustly attacked and also experienced the total unpredictability of the other's rage. Her *unconscious communication of feelings produced a change in my sense of self.* I emphasize again, this is a process that is immediate, unconscious, and involuntary.

An affective experience is transferred from the patient's inner world into the mind of the analyst. What are transferred are not pure feelings but feelings embedded in a context of specific meaning. The meaning in this instance derives from the patient's memory of a disturbing and unassimilated relationship with her father. This phenomenon is primitive in that the feelings invoked are not subject to judgment and are outside of the agency of the self. In projective identification, intense feelings are unconsciously communicated with a semantic specificity that precludes ambiguity and constricts the imagination. How this process works is simply not known.

Fantasies That Constrict the Imagination

Fantasy is an omnibus term that includes a whole array of different phenomena.[4] When one thinks of a fantasy, one may refer to a transitory daydream, a will-o'-the-wisp of thought that enters in and out of consciousness, or a dominating, embedded belief. As the psychoanalyst Ethel Person (1995) observed, most of us are unaware of the extent to which we devote our thoughts to daydreams and fantasies. We recognize that fantasizing assumes a multitude of forms and functions. Grandiose fantasies of the self may compensate for a deep sense of inadequacy; a lonely child may create a fantasy companion or an adult may create a world of fantasy into which they can escape when reality becomes impossible to endure. It is well known that fantasizing can provide alternative worlds.

A certain class of fantasies does not expand or transform the imagination but constricts it. When present, such fantasies can exert an organizing effect on the individual's life by contributing to a belief system that seriously limits his options and choices. These fantasies can justifiably be described as malignant; they appear to be intractable, whether or not they are conscious or unconscious. Freud was unduly optimistic with regard to the therapeutic value of interpretation that rendered an unconscious fantasy conscious. He had too much faith in the rationalizing power of language. It is possible for a fantasy to dominate one's life, and it does not matter whether such a fantasy is conscious or unconscious.

One such malignant fantasy is the belief that love is destructive: that loving another will ultimately harm the other or lead to his or her death; or, in the opposite direction, that one will be destroyed by the other's love. Because of individual differences and the multiplicity of determinants, there can be no straightforward single explanation for the origin of this belief that love is destructive. For some, it would appear that the metaphoric interpretation of intense feeling plays a significant role. For example, in some individuals, passion may be interpreted as an overwhelming intense heat, a fire within the body that is all consuming and therefore implicitly destructive. If such intense feelings can destroy the self, the other can also be destroyed. Operatic drama provides many instances of those who are destroyed by love—a prime example would be the mythic love-death of Tristan and Isolde.

An embedded fantasy that one's love is dangerous may have tragic consequences. Under the sway of such a fantasy, one is forced to avoid intimate relationships. Not surprisingly, the fantasy that love is destructive is an organizing belief in the so-called schizoid personality, whose sufferers are withdrawn, isolated, and aloof (Fairbairn 1952).

A malignant fantasy of this sort can also be described as a steady state resistant to change. Nonlinear dynamic-systems theory contains very attractive metaphors that describe systems resistant to change; such systems are referred to as *basins of attraction*.[5] The basin of attraction describes a stable state based on the analogy of a ball rolling to the bottom of a bowl no matter where in the bowl it was originally dropped. The steady state that the ball achieves after it rolls to the bottom of a bowl results from the confluence of a multiplicity of factors derived from many systems. The fantasy that one's love is destructive can be described as such a *malignant basin of attraction*. No matter where one starts, one extracts the same meaning from experience. Such a fantasy directs one's imagination.

In chapter 4, I showed how a primal metaphor, the body as a container, can contribute to a guilt-producing fantasy. Such a fantasy can also function as a malignant basin of attraction. The primary metaphor of the body as a container leads to the following image: *when something "good" is taken into the body/self, it is "all gone" and not available to other members of the family.* "Good" within the family is viewed as a zero-sum game. This embedded fantasy will limit what the individual is able to have for oneself. For to have something "good" means that it is taken away from other family members.

Defining Imagination

Imagination seems to be ubiquitous. Do we consider everything that occurs in our head, in the absence of sensory input, imagination? Does imagination include everything that is mental? If not, what then are its limits and boundaries?

How do we define imagination? Aristotle defined imagination as a "sensation without matter" (see Aristotle on imagination in chapter 5). He said, "Imagination is not the same as perception, but imagination cannot occur without perception" (Aristotle 1986, p. 198). This is also true for memory. Imagination is not possible without memory, but neither is memory possible without imagination. As Bartlett famously wrote, "Remembering is not the re-excitation of innumerable fixed, lifeless and fragmentary traces. It is an *imaginative* construction, or a construction built out of the relation of our attitude towards a whole active mass of organized past reactions or experience" (1932; my emphasis).

The term *imagination,* like the term *fantasy,* includes a multitude of different phenomena. Imagination may refer to the scenes that we construct in our minds as we read a novel, or to the lustful, angry, or frightening thoughts and images that occasionally enter into our consciousness. These very different experiences are all described as products of our imagination. But imagination is also an unconscious process, an unconscious potentiality. This unconscious process generates fantasies when we are awake as well as dreams when we are asleep. Coleridge likened this unconscious process to a "master-current" below the surface of consciousness (1817, p. 242; see the epigraph to this chapter).

We know through introspection that imagination has qualities of its own that distinguish it from perception and memory: we usually can distinguish what we imagine from what we perceive and remember, although memory at times may be indistinguishable from imagination. What specifically characterizes imagination? You will recall that Castoriadis asserted that it is not our capacity for reason but our radical imagination that makes us uniquely human. I have suggested that other species experience visual images but that we are unique in our capacity for *interpretive* imagining.

Kant differentiated imagination from other mental functions in his *Critique of Pure Reason* (1787). He described two broad categories of imagination, which he called (not very helpfully) *productive* and *reproductive*. Productive imagination refers to the synthetic function of thought that brings together disparate elements and ideas by means of schemata. This essential aspect of imagination consists of a *synthesis* of disparate elements. Let us assume, although Kant did not use the term *unconscious*, that this *productive* imagination functions by means of unconscious schemata. The philosopher Mark Johnson (1987, p. 74), who with George Lakoff founded cognitive linguistics, acknowledges that their idea of an unconscious metaphoric process was derived from Kant's theory of the productive imagination.[6] There are important differences between Kant's productive imagination and the unconscious metaphoric process that I have described in the previous chapters. For Kant believed that the *productive imagination* was an a priori given that is present in the mind apart from experience. In contrast to what we think today, Kant's a priori productive imagination was impersonal and not the private, unique creation of the individual. Kant's other category, *reproductive imagination*, in contrast, is based on the experience of the individual (and the "laws" of association) and does represent a uniquely personal imagination.

Kant believed that shared schemata are formed by a priori rules.[7] It made possible a shared imagination that resulted in scientific knowledge. Kant's conception of a mind that imposes its categories upon the world without itself being altered by the world is very far removed from our pragmatic, ecological point of view. One can retain Kant's idea of imagination as an unconscious synthetic process, but one must add that it is a process that utilizes metaphor and is based on the experience of the individual.[8]

Kant has shown that concepts and categories are mental constructions that are distinctly separate from the specificity of an image. *An image has the quality of being differentiated, in contrast to concepts and categories.* My image of my large black poodle Natasha is differentiated from all other dogs and is quite unlike thinking about the category "dog." Although Kant would not agree, we may arrive at categories by means of the imagination, but the category itself is logically, and most probably neurologically, distinct from the imagination. Using a different illustration, Kant said, "Indeed it is schemata, not images of objects, which underlie our pure sensible concepts. No image can ever be adequate to the concept of the triangle in general. It would never attain that universality of the concept which renders it valid for all triangles" (1787, p. 182).

The Selection of Images from the Stream of Consciousness

The geneticist R. C. Lewontin asks, What is the "I" that selects and brings thoughts and images to one's conscious attention? Here is an excerpt from his review of Changeux's *Neuronal Man* (1997), which appeared in the *New York Review of Books:*

The heart of the problem of mind and brain is the shift of consciousness by what appears to us to be a willful act. As I tire of writing, I think first of the impending visit of a friend, then I strain to hear which Scarlatti sonata my wife is practicing, and then I return again to think about the relation of ego and mental images. I have passed among three very different mental states all under the control of the willful "I." Some kind of information about all these states must all the while have been resident in my *brain,* but only one at a time was in my *mind.* What chooses among them? "I" [do]. The central problem remains for neurobiology: What is "I"? (Lewontin 1985)

This self-selection of images that Lewontin illustrates could be described as a defining characteristic of consciousness. In the two chapters that follow, I will examine this selective process and its relation to feelings.

7   The Uniqueness of Human Feelings

A feeling is merely the material quality of a mental sign.

C. S. Peirce

When our species acquired a capacity for metaphor and language, it changed how we feel: with the acquisition of metaphor, feelings could be interpreted. This is a uniquely human attribute. Yet our limbic system, the emotional brain, is of ancient origin, which means that human emotions cannot be entirely unique. In contrast to other primates, we can inhibit our expression of feelings, but we are also subject, as they are, to uncontrollable rages and sudden erotic impulses. What, then, is distinctive about human emotion? One obvious difference between chimpanzees and ourselves is our ability to transform our emotions—a process that Freud described as sublimation. Sublimation is uniquely human, but on the other hand, emotions in ourselves, as well as in other species, function as internal monitors of homeostasis and markers of value. These are some of the issues that I will discuss in this chapter.

The Concept of the Limbic System

Paul MacLean introduced the term *limbic system* in 1952 (see MacLean 1949, 1990). MacLean, who was influenced by psychoanalytic theory, attempted to separate the emotional brain from other components and to place those structures within an evolutionary context. The phrase *limbic system* represents a synthetic concept in which an old term introduced by Pierre Paul Broca, in the nineteenth century, was placed in a new perspective. Broca described a ring of tissue on the medial cerebral hemisphere, which he called le *grande lobe limbique*. *Limbique* means border or fringe. Later this ring came to be called the old brain or the rhinencephelon—the nose brain. But in 1930 James Papez showed that Broca's limbic lobe, the rhinencephelon with its olfactory inputs, was primarily part of a circuitry that was functionally related to emotion.[1] Papez advanced the theory that "the hypothalamus, the anterior thalmic nuclei, the cingulate gyrus, the hippocampus, and their connections constitute a harmonious mechanism which may elaborate the functions of central emotion as well as participate in emotional expression" (MacLean 1949). MacLean revitalized Papez's theory as well as Broca's old term by calling Papez's ensemble of structures "the limbic system."

There is, however, no agreement among authorities as to what structures constitute the limbic system and no agreement as to its phylogenetic significance. Most neuroscientists, such as the neuroanatomists Nauta and Feirtag (1986), would include in the limbic system the hypothalamus, the hippocampus, the amygdala, and those cortical areas that Broca described, as well as the entorhinal cortex adjacent to the hippocampus. Panksepp (1998a) would also include the midbrain, specifically, the mesencephalic reticular formation and the periaqueductal gray (PAG). As an example of the difference of opinion regarding phylogeny, MacLean (1990) claims that the limbic system coincides with the old mammalian brain, whereas Freeman (1999b) believes that the limbic system coincides with the salamander's forebrain. It should also be added that there is some current debate regarding the legitimacy of the limbic system as a concept. LeDoux believes that the neural circuits that the concept describes are imprecise and that the concept has "unwarranted functional (emotional) implications and should be discarded" (1996, p. 101). Panksepp (1998a), on the other hand, believes LeDoux's rejection of the limbic system as a concept to be totally misguided. My own view is that the limbic system is a heuristically necessary part of the "conceptual" nervous system, as it allows us to think of the evolution of emotion as a separate and distinct function of the mind/brain.

There is recent evidence that a limbic system can be found in protovertebrates. A rudimentary limbic system has been observed in the lancelet, a primitive protovertebrate and marine organism that is a relative of the lamprey (Zimmer 2000). The evolution of the limbic system may be related to the organism's need to monitor its internal states as preparation for motor action in the environment. The appearance of the limbic system in the lancelet seems to have coincided with the animal's transition from passive feeding to predatory behavior. For unlike the passive feeder, the predatory animal must be prepared to react to internal signals that prime the animal to either fight or flee (Zimmer 2000). It would appear that insects are programmed to fight or flee in a more robotic manner that precludes the need for a limbic system or, for that matter, consciousness.

This would suggest that the origin of emotions may be related to the need for the individual animal to mobilize its bodily responses *as a whole*. This holistic response presages the development of self and consciousness. The need for the psychological coherence of the self may reflect this ancient physiological requirement. Panksepp described this holistic response as "primal state spaces" generated by emotional value systems (2000). The limbic system monitors and responds to the requirements for homeostasis; emotions provide the appropriate internal signals that mobilize the individual to either fight or flee.

Paul MacLean (1990) speculated that the limbic system might be designed to amplify or lower the intensity of feelings involved in guiding the behaviors required for self-preservation. I have adopted the convention (suggested in Damasio 1999) of differentiating the terms *feeling* and *emotion:* only conscious individuals feel, whereas it is highly probable that *emotions* existed before the evolution of consciousness. Emotions can monitor and transmit information concerning the individual's vital needs without consciousness. As emotions are keyed to the regulation of homeostasis, they transmit and inform one of value. So it is a reasonable assumption that unconscious *emotions*, functioning as internal automatic signals, were present long before consciousness itself evolved. As an inheritance from this older biological self, the psychological self demonstrates a similar need for coherence.

What Is Unique about Human Feelings?

The fact that animals have feelings has long been an unquestioned assumption of folk psychology (but this is not an assumption shared by all cognitive scientists). But folk psychology also believes that only humans have the capacity to restrain the expression of their emotions. Philosophers for several millennia have speculated about the difference between animal and human emotion. As I noted earlier, according to St. Thomas Aquinas, the existence of free will is the feature that distinguishes human and animal emotion. He said, "Sheep flee the wolf because they judge it dangerous, but the judgment is not free but imposed on them by nature" (Aquinas 1264, p. 99). Aquinas believed that the immediacy of the animal's response indicates that they lack free will and therefore are not able to judge what is good, for only men have minds endowed with free will and with it the capacity to make moral judgments. Aquinas thought that our ability to reason and arrive at moral judgments explains our capacity for emotional delay. This idea is consistent with the age-old assumption that there is, within us, a fundamental opposition between our animal passions and human reason.

For Spinoza, our inability to moderate and restrain our emotions indicates a "human bondage." He wrote, "An affect which is called a passion of the mind is a confused idea, by which the mind affirms of its body . . . , which when it is given determines the mind to think of this rather than that. Man's lack of power to moderate and restrain the affects I call bondage. For the man who is subject to affects is under the control not of himself but of fortune" (Spinoza 1675, pp. 196–197).

Even Freud was influenced by the supposition that affects and reason are opposing forces, when he proposed a functional division of the mind into an irrational id and a reasoning ego. This functional distinction between feeling and reason continues to be maintained by some cognitive psychologists and neuroscientists who view cognition and emotion as entirely separate faculties of the mind.[2] Damasio (1994), who emphasizes the unity of emotion and cognition, is an exception. Although there is this ancient tradition that separates "animal" passions from human reason, we also know that feelings and "reason" are inseparable in health, but can become separate in pathological states.

For example, there is a rare neurological disorder called Capgras' syndrome, where the victim of this illness will claim, "This person is not my wife. She's either an imposter or a double." Capgras' syndrome is a neurological, rather than a psychiatric, illness: the individual is suffering not from a delusion but from a brain lesion. The neurologist Ramachandran offers the explanation that Capgras' syndrome reflects a brain lesion where there is a disconnect between the limbic system and the area in the temporal lobe that is activated when we recognize faces (see Ramachandran and Blakeslee 1998). To identify a person, it is not enough to recognize who they are: we must also *feel* who they are. In health there is always a feeling component in perceiving.

Darwin assumed that there are continuities between the expression of emotion in animals and the expression of emotion in human beings. Darwin noted that humans and animals are aroused by the same primordial emotions of fear and rage (1872). In addition, intelligent mammals, such as monkeys and dogs, share with us what he called more complex emotions, such as jealousy and curiosity. From this it may be inferred that evolution has preserved homologous brain structures that generate the expression of similar, if not identical, emotions.

Joseph LeDoux (1996) has shown that the amygdala mediates the emotion of fear in rats. Panksepp (1998a) describes a "fear circuit" in animals involving the amygdala, hypothalamus, and midbrain (PAG). The fact that the amygdala is fully developed in the newborn of many vertebrate species suggests that the emotion of fear is essential for survival—the newborn gazelle will automatically, and without instruction from its mother, flee from the lion. There is evidence to support the inference that the amygdala helps mediate fearful emotion in humans as well. Experiments using the noninvasive technique of fMRI with human subjects have shown that the amygdala is also activated as a response to the exposure of fearful faces, but not in response to neutral faces (Breiter et al. 1996). These experiments have shown that the amygdala responds not only to fearful faces but also to happy faces.

The amygdala may activate the emotion of fear in both rats and men, but again we must be reminded that metaphor and language interpret feelings, which results in a divergence between humans and other species. This is reflected in the distinction between *anxiety* and *fear*. Fear is a universal feeling present in all mammals, whereas anxiety can be aroused by means of metaphoric associations and is in this sense uniquely human. We share the emotion of fear with other species but only human beings experience anxiety. Freud adopted this linguistic convention of distinguishing the terms *fear* and *anxiety*. He believed that fear refers to real danger whereas anxiety is an internal signal of danger embedded in specified associations that can be symbolized. For example, Little Hans' phobia that a horse would bite him was based on the metaphoric correspondence between the horse and his father and reflected little Hans' peculiar life history.

Anxiety, unlike fear, can be metaphorically transformed into an erotic feeling, and an erotic feeling, in turn, can be transformed into anxiety. The singularly human cognitive capacity for creating metaphors enables us to conflate anxiety and sexual arousal. This is one of the reasons that we enjoy horror movies. Our capacity to transform "base" emotions into "higher" feelings Freud called sublimation, which he viewed as man's greatest achievement, an achievement that made civilization possible. But the nature of sublimation itself, as we shall see, remains particularly mysterious.

Our unique linguistic, imaginative, and symbolic capacities provide a *degree of freedom* from the exigent demands of our internal and external environments. Chimpanzees, our genetically closest relative, when emotionally aroused, cannot suppress their vocal cries. Jane Goodall writes, "Chimpanzee vocalizations are closely tied to emotion. The production of a sound in the absence of the appropriate emotional state seems to be an almost impossible task for a chimpanzee" (cited in Lieberman 1991). Goodall continues, "On one occasion when Figan [a chimpanzee at the Gombe Stream Reservation] was an adolescent, he waited in camp until the senior males had left and we were able to give him some bananas (he had had none before). His excited food calls quickly brought the big males racing back and Figan lost his fruit. A few days later he waited behind again, and once more received his bananas. He made no loud sounds, but the calls could be heard deep in his throat, almost causing him to gag."

The linguist Derek Bickerton (1995) believes that it is primarily language that enables the human being to go off line. He contrasts two basic modes of thinking that he calls on-line thinking and off-line thinking. On-line thinking focuses upon the immediate environment. On-line thinking can occur only in terms of the neural responses elicited by the presence of external objects. In contrast, off-line thinking, dependent on language, involves "computations" carried out in the absence of the object, utilizing an internal "repre-sentation" of the object. This internalization, he believes, allows us to go off line. He believes that it is language, and not our capacity for moral judgment, as Aquinas thought, that allows us to delay our emotional response to environ-mental inputs. Bickerton argues that it is not only language, but more specifically syntax, that allows us to go off line. He acknowledges that some primates and dolphins have protolanguages, but their languages lack the syntactic struc-ture that would enable them to go off line.

Play, Emotions, and the Complexity of Consciousness

This rigidity and inflexibility of an emotional response, the inability to delay the expression of emotion that Figan dis-played when he received the bananas, would not appear in a different context, one in which vital needs were not at risk. It would be different if Figan were simply playing with ba-nanas. When animals are at play, emotions have a different valence, and threatening gestures do not carry the same import.

Playful behavior characterizes all mammalian species. In the transition from reptiles to mammals MacLean (1990) noted three differentiating behavioral developments: (1) nursing and attachment behavior, (2) the vocal communi-cation necessary for maintaining attachment, and finally, (3) play. The significance of play has been underestimated by most neuroscientists. An exception is Jaak Panksepp (1998a), who investigated the feeling systems associated with play in mammals. Although the neurophysiology of play is virtually unexplored, Panksepp suggested that the joyful and pleasurable feelings associated with play may have their own neural circuitry. Whether this proves to be true or not, it is evident that play provides a different context that changes the animal's emotional responses so that emotions do not result in a predetermined fixed pattern of actions.

Gregory Bateson (1972) observed animals playing in a zoo and wondered how the animals understand that a threatening gesture or an aggressive move is not really intended. Does the animal recognize some "mood signs" to indicate "This is only a game"? Bateson suggested that playing exists within a *frame*, a global context that separates play from other aspects of ordinary life. Feelings expressed within this context of the playing frame would have a different meaning as compared to the expression of emotions in life outside of the frame. Bateson saw the analogy of the frame to the psychotherapeutic setup that can be analogized to a game with its recognized rules. I have commented on the use of frames in psychoanalytic treatment in *Other Times, Other Realities* (Modell 1990). The frame of treatment may provide the measure of safety that enables expression of feeling that may not be possible outside of the frame. It would appear that the expression of emotion in animals, as in humans, is influenced by the overall environmental context. The context of play presumes a measure of safety, so feelings are at least temporarily delinked from the homeostatic requirements of survival. The context of the environmental surround thus influences the complexity of consciousness. Safe environments expand consciousness.

Games have an "as if" quality that separates the actions that occur within the game from the actions of ordinary life. I have described all of this in greater detail in *Other Times, Other Realities* (Modell 1990). When there are intense transference and countertransference feelings, this "as if" quality of the game may be temporarily suspended, resulting in a loss of the complexity of consciousness. In the treatment frame, both analyst and patient may be aware of themselves as individuals, as they are in ordinary life, and they are also conscious of the social role that they occupy within the frame of the treatment game, that of patient and therapist. At the same time, there is a possibility that as a consequence of metonymy, the other may be imaginatively associated with significant persons from one's past. This can be described as a complex consciousness encompassing multiple levels of reality, all of which can be simultaneously held in consciousness. To maintain awareness of these different levels of consciousness requires an ambience of safety. As with play, the limbic system is temporarily off line with regard to vital needs.

When watching a movie or a play, our vital interests are not at risk. The theater and movies can also be thought of as a frame, analogous to play, that provides a context that separates experience within the frame from feelings customarily felt outside of the frame. Some people who cannot cry in ordinary life are able to cry when watching a movie. The psychoanalyst Donald Kaplan (1993) cited a study of the art of acting in which it was noted that we can more easily identify with actors because we are not threatened, as in life, by the otherness of other people. Therefore, we can respond to the uniqueness of their characters with a greater sense of autonomy than we may experience in real life. Actors cannot harm us, because they make no demands on us: we are not obligated to save Desdemona from Othello, because we can't. Freud made an essentially similar observation in his little-known paper "Psychopathic characters on the stage" (1906), where he noted that as a spectator one takes pleasure in the illusion of sharing in the suffering of the actor because we know that it is only a game.

The Enigma of "Sublimation"

In a broader context, sublimation can be seen as an aspect of the corporeal imagination. As described earlier, feelings, by means of metaphor, can be displaced, conflated, and transformed. I find *sublimation* to be an obscure and somewhat muddled concept that encompasses two different ideas. Our direct response to works of art, which may consist of joy, anxiety, sadness, disgust, anger, and so forth, can be thought of as a form of sublimation The term *sublimation* refers not only to the awakening of these aesthetic feelings but also to the process that transforms these feelings into something that is deemed to be "higher," to say, culturally valuable. Understanding the details of this process remains a challenging problem.

Originally, the term *sublimation* referred to the method used by an alchemist in which a "base" metal is heated to yield something "higher" or more *sublime*. Freud retained the idea of transforming something base into something higher or sublime by defining sublimation as the transformation of the "base" instinct eros into "higher" cultural achievements.[3] The alchemist, through sublimation, attempted to transform a base metal into gold. A familiar Freudian example of sublimation would be the fact that a child's interest in feces can be transformed, can be sublimated, into an adult's interest in money. Sublimation, according to Freud, consists of the diversion of a partial drive or instinct from its original aim. When Freud thought of sublimation as a diversion and transformation of eros, he was combining both his belief in the synthetic function of the libido with the romantic notion that sexual energy is the primordial force behind our species' highest achievements.

Freud's best known illustration of sublimation can be found in his essay on Leonardo de Vinci, where Freud described how Leonardo's voyeuristic, childish sexual curiosity was transformed into scientific curiosity. Freud wrote, "The child's sexual impulses are powerful enough to sexualize thinking itself and to color intellectual operations with pleasure and anxiety that belong to sexual processes proper. Here an investigation becomes a sexual activity, and the feeling that comes from settling things in one's mind and explaining them replaces sexual satisfaction" (1910). Freud could have been talking about himself.

Freud relied on instinct theory to explain sublimation. He understood sublimation to result from a substitution of a "desexualized" aim for a directly erotic aim. But in view of an individual's autonomous corporeal imagination, it would be difficult to maintain a belief in universal entities such as instincts or drives, for each individual interprets the feelings that such "drives" generate in their own particular manner. The idea of "desexualized" instincts cannot account for sublimation. The transformation of feeling, which is at the heart of sublimation, would not be possible without an autonomous metaphoric process. Again, it is to metaphor, rather than instinct, that we must turn in seeking an explanation of sublimation.

The Interpretation of Sensations

In attempting to understand how feelings can be "sublimated" by means of metaphor, I have found it useful to assume that there is an initial "raw" bodily sensation, which, when interpreted, becomes a feeling.[4] *Let us hypothesize that an unconscious metaphoric process interprets sensations, which we then experience as feelings.*[5] *I suggest that raw sensations are interpreted by unconscious processes entailing memory and metaphor, the results of which are then experienced as feelings.* This method provides a "raw" sensation with contextual information. This theory assumes that internal sensations are processed in a manner analogous to the perception of external objects.

That perception can be thought of as the interpretation of sensation receives some support in neuroscience from Walter Freeman's (1999b) investigation of olfaction in rabbits. He observed that during the stage of sensation, which consists of the excitation of the receptor cells in the nose, there is no extraction of information or meaning. Perception occurs "behind" the receptor cells; it is there that the olfactory bulb and the brain construct meaning. Freeman sees the "raw" olfactory sensation as information that is fleeting and evanescent. He states, "The entire body of the individual's experience is collapsed within a few milliseconds in its engagement with a sample from the world. The sense data are transcended and expunged so as to minimize clutter" (Freeman, personal communication). After the sensation is interpreted, the sensory surface is wiped clean. Freeman's research confirms an insight of Freud's described in his paper "A note upon the 'mystic writing pad'" (1925), where he speculated that the perceptual surface of consciousness (sensation) needs to be constantly refreshed by deletion, that "unlimited receptive capacity and memory are mutually exclusive."

These observations reinforce the supposition that different cerebral domains operate in accordance with different rules. Employing this supposition, I would propose that the perception of feelings utilizes different neural rules as compared, for example, to visual perception. Visual perception, in contrast to the perception of feelings, is lawful and not subject to interpretation by the individual. The cognitive scientist Donald Hoffman (1998) described how we construct visual worlds from ambiguous images by means of certain specified, impersonal rules. In contrast, the perception of feelings relies on the corporeal imagination, which in turn is determined by the history of the self.

You may question whether it is possible to experience a bodily sensation that is devoid of any context. Is this idea anything more than a thought experiment? Can we experience an erotic sensation before it is interpreted and provided with a memorial context? Whether or not such raw sensations can in fact be introspected, let us at least consider this as a possibility. Mark Solms and Edward Nersessian, in their account of Freud's affect theory (Solms and Nersessian 1999), remind us that Freud conceptualized feelings as the equivalent and counterpart of sensory qualia, such as seeing the color red. We need to be reminded again that consciousness is Janus-faced. Consciousness has an internal perceptual surface that is directed towards the body. Feelings are the sensations, arising from within the body, analogous to the sensations provided by those sensory portals that receive their inputs from the external world.

Perception of a feeling, in contrast to *sensation*, would consist then of a process in which the sensation is linked to memory and metaphor, providing it with contextual information. Metaphor mediates, categorizes, and thus organizes the perception of bodily sensations.

Metaphor, in addition to the cognitive function of interpreting sensations, may contribute to a simple *displacement* of feeling. Metaphor transfers meaning between dissimilar domains, which allows for the play of similarity and difference. Anxiety and sexual arousal are experienced as similar and dissimilar forms of excitement, so by means of meta-phor someone can experience the eroticization of anxiety. It may be arbitrary whether one describes this as a sublima-tion. Whether one recognizes a feeling as sublimated may depend on whether feelings are merely conflated or actually transformed. Perhaps the transformation of feeling reflects a more complex interpretation of sensation. In any case, sub-limation can be better understood as a complex interpreta-tion of feeling, rather than as a *desexualization of instinct,* as Freud believed.

The distinction between metaphoric *transfer* and meta-phoric *transformation* of feeling can be illustrated if we turn to psychopathology. Psychopathology can be viewed as na-ture's experiment in which a vital component is subtracted or removed, as in a thought experiment. Not infrequently, when someone is afflicted with schizophrenia, there is a cog-nitive deficit in which the patient suffers from a loss of the transformative power of metaphor. The British psychoana-lyst Hanna Segal gave the following account of a schizo-phrenic patient in a mental hospital: "He was once asked by his doctor why it was that since his illness he had stopped playing the violin? He replied with some violence: 'Why? do you expect me to masturbate in public?' " (1957). I can recall a similar observation regarding a patient who was severely inhibited in the use of his intellect. Unlike Hanna Segal's patient, he was not in any sense psychotic, yet he believed that the pleasure and excitement that he could ob-tain from using his mind was forbidden to him as if it were similar to masturbation. In both these examples there was a sensation of pleasurable excitement, in one case from play-ing a musical instrument, in the other from using one's mind. The *sensation* of pleasurable excitement became a *feel-ing* when it was conflated by means of a metaphoric similarity. Because of this similarity, pleasure from the use of the body/mind was conflated with the memory of the sensations associated with masturbation. An unconscious metaphoric process condensed the actions of playing the violin, using one's mind, and stroking one's penis. Sensation was processed by metaphor to produce a feeling that was lacking in complexity, in contrast to a more multifaceted metaphorization of feeling.

The failure of sublimation in these examples have been customarily described as evidence of concrete thinking, a loss of a capacity for abstract thought, or an impairment of the symbolic function.[6] I would understand this failure of sublimation as a loss of perceptual complexity. As metaphor is defined as the transfer of meaning between different domains, it would be not quite accurate to describe these examples as a failure of the symbolic function or an absence of the use of metaphor. The failure of sublimation in these examples represents a constriction of interpretation that would otherwise *transform sensation*. This inability to transform raw sensations appears to be the result of a cognitive failure, a constriction of the open web of associations generated by metaphor. In health, metaphor evokes a plurality of meaning, what linguists call *polysemy*. Metaphor also allows for a play of similarity and difference, resulting in a complex perception of a feeling. The schizophrenic patient who equated his violin with his penis suffered, as do traumatized patients, from a cognitive deficit resulting in the degradation of an unconscious metaphoric process.

The Semiotics of Feeling

I have suggested that the difference between a metaphoric process that merely *transfers* meaning and a metaphoric process that *transforms* meaning can be attributed to the contextual complexity that has been added to perception. The web of associations may be enlarged or constricted by metaphor and metonymy, so that perception comes to interpret sensation. If we think of sensations as internal signs that can be cognitively transformed by interpretation, these ideas are similar to the semiotic theory proposed by the philosopher Charles Sanders Peirce (1910). Peirce described three logical categories of signs: iconic, indexical, and symbolic. An iconic sign is based on similarity alone—the patient who thought he was masturbating when he played the violin interpreted the violin as an extension of his body, an iconic sign of the penis. Indexical signs are based on contiguity. When the wind changes the direction of a weather vane as the wind "touches" the weather vane, the weather vane itself becomes a sign of the wind. Similarly, the rise of the column of mercury in a thermometer is a sign of a rise in temperature. Indexical signs *point*. Metonymic associations can also be seen as indexical signs, as the part points to the whole. As I described earlier, a metonymic association can evoke, that is to say point to, an entire gestalt of a former affective experience. In Peirce's terminology, a metaphoric process that merely transfers meaning may be both iconic and indexical. Peirce understood the third term *symbol* to refer to a conventional interpretation of a sign. The cartoon outline of a man that is attached to the door of the men's lavatory would be an example of Peirce's notion of a symbol. For Peirce, feelings are signs that are subject to semiotic interpretations at different levels of complexity.[7] This should prove to be a useful way of thinking about sublimation.

Not only did Peirce insist that feelings are subject to interpretation, but also what he described as "feelings" are very similar to raw sensations. Peirce writes, "The elementary phenomena of mind fall into three categories. First, we have Feelings, comprising all that is immediately present, such as pain, blue, cheerfulness. . . . A feeling is a state of mind having its own living qualities independent of any other state of mind" (1891, p. 150).

Peirce's proposal that feelings are immediately present without reference to anything else (a quality for which he created the neologism "firstness") is a good definition of a "raw" sensation. As the psychoanalyst John Muller (2000) commented, Peirce's notion is that feelings are immediately present and are experienced as a form of "coerced mirroring" that leads to action. Peirce thus implied that the interpretation of a feeling can be forced and involuntary.

Once More, Are Human Feelings Unique?

I began this chapter describing the limbic system, which generates emotions. This structural homology between ourselves and other species suggests both that emotional systems are of ancient origin and that human emotions cannot be unique. At the close of this chapter I described theories suggesting that in our species, sensations are interpreted and become feelings as a consequence of a metaphoric process. This cognitive tool can explain the plasticity of human feeling and the fact that feelings can be sublimated. We share with other species a similar emotional brain to which has been added a specifically human cognitive capacity that changes how we feel.

8   Feelings and Value

Meaning is embodied in our total affective interest in the world.
Giambattista Vico

The absence of meaning in life is excruciatingly painful: it is as if one were psychically dead; to find life meaningful is to be attached to life. When clinicians encounter patients who suffer from the conviction that their lives are empty, futile, and meaningless, they recognize this as a symptom of an illness. When feelings have become disassociated from the self, the self in turn is felt to be empty and dead, as if there were nothing there. There is an evident intimate connection between feelings, values, and the experience of self. Feelings assign value to what is meaningful.

In this chapter I will examine this essential relationship between feelings, meaning, and the self. Again, what I plan to consider here is the meaning of *experience,* which is by definition personal meaning. This entails a bracketing of the social construction of meaning (religion and the like). In addition, this discussion will also bracket the philosopher's inquiry into the shared conventional meaning of language. In

chapter 1, I alluded to a puzzle that has so occupied philosophers: the distinction between personal, idiosyncratic meaning, meaning created by individual selves, on one hand,
and, on the other, ready-made, socially constructed conventional meaning. Jerome Bruner (1990) said that meaning is
shaped by culture but restrained by biology. As we are concerned here with a biology of meaning, I have adopted what
has been called an *internalist* view, the belief that meaning
is constructed from within. Meaning stops at the skin.[1]

Walter Freeman asserts that meaning is always solipsistic,
that each individual perceives sensations in their own
unique fashion: "All that brains can know has been synthe-
sized within themselves, in the form of hypotheses about
the world and the outcomes of their own tests of the hypotheses. This is the neurobiological basis for the solipsistic isola-
tion that separates the qualia of each person from the
experiences of everyone else" (1999b, p. 93).

In the *Private Self* (1993) I too presented a view of the self
that is biased in an internalist direction. Although we depend on others for self-affirmation, we essentially create
ourselves, bootstrap ourselves, from within and make idiosyncratic, private use of shared concepts and values.

It may be useful, before proceeding further, to review the
relation between feelings and value that I discussed earlier:
(1) The world is an unlabeled place that we categorize by
selecting what is of value and interest to us. This can be
expressed as *value-driven selection*. (2) Feeling and emotion
are markers of value. I have adopted the convention of distinguishing emotions from feeling: emotions refer to the
neurophysiological processes from which feelings are derived. Emotions, in contrast to feelings, are unconscious.
(3) Emotional memories, by means of metaphoric associa-

tions, form unconscious categories that are the source of *potential* meaning. (4) Metaphor therefore is the interpreter or organizer of unconscious emotional categories. (5) Internal sensations can also be interpreted by an unconscious metaphoric process.

Individual and Shared States of Consciousness

When we consider those items that are selected for conscious awareness, we need to contrast the mutually shared aspects of consciousness from the private and personal aspects of consciousness. Let us imagine a scene in which two people are in a therapist's office. Both individuals are conscious of the same view. They perceive the same desk, couch, carpet, books; if they look through the windows, they see the sunlight and the movement of the trees. They hear the same street noises: the sound of passing cars, the barking of a dog. This can be described as an "objective" consciousness of socially shared perceptions and experiences. But at the same time the patient and the therapist are both conscious of their own associations, daydreams, and fantasies—items of consciousness that are selected by their individual selves and are completely idiosyncratic. These items of consciousness are not part of a common objective consciousness. Their selection depends on the individual's own history and conscious and unconscious intentionalities. This private aspect of consciousness is usually referred to as a consciousness of an *inner world,* which includes a consciousness of internal dialogues.[2] Ernest Schactel (1959) described this consciousness of the inner world as *auto-centric* perception, in contrast to the so-called "objective" consciousness of shared perceptions. This distinction between autocentric perception and objective perception shows that personal selection is limited to only a sector of consciousness.

William James believed that selection is a defining characteristic of consciousness, that consciousness is at all times primarily a selecting agency (1890, p. 139).[3] This is beautifully illustrated by the following quotation from William James' *Principles of Psychology:*

Millions of items of the outward order are present to my senses which never properly enter into my experience. Why? Because they have no *interest* for me; *my experience is what I agree to intend to.* Only those items which I notice shape my mind—without selective interest, experience is an utter chaos. Interest alone gives accent and emphasis, lighting and shade, background and foreground— intelligible perspectives in a word. It varies in every creature, but without it the consciousness of every creature would be a gray chaotic indiscriminateness, impossible for us even to conceive. (1890, vol. 1, p. 402)

Although James did not use the term *value,* value is implicit in the analogy James uses in following passage, where he asks, *"Can consciousness increase its efficiency by loading its dice?"*

Loading its dice would mean bringing a more or less constant pressure to bear in favor of *those* of its performances which makes for the most permanent interests of the brain's owner; it would mean a constant inhibition of the tendencies to stray aside. Well, just such pressure and such inhibition are what consciousness *seems* to be exerting all the while. And the interests in whose favor it seems to exert them are *its* interests and its alone, interests which it *creates,* and which for it would have no status in the realm of being whatever. Consciousness seems to itself to be a *fighter for ends.* Its powers of cognition are mainly subservient to those ends, discerning which facts further them and which do not. (James 1890, vol. 1, p. 140)

Value and Cathexis

When James spoke of consciousness increasing its efficiency by loading its dice, had he been alive today he might have described its loading its dice as an expression of *value*, as probabilistic expectancies. Many in the neuroscience community have adopted the term *value*, familiar to moral philosophers, to denote the salience implicit in emotion and feeling. I am not sure who was the first to introduce this term into neuroscience, but the concept of value is central to Edelman's theory of neuronal selection. As with James' term *loaded dice, value* implies a bias derived ultimately from the constraints of evolution and resulting in a probabilistic expectancy. In Edelman's theory, the homeostatic requirements of the individual exert a bias on memory and perception. Value is a necessary component of the selection process that occurs within reentry. (*Reentry* is a term introduced by Edelman [1987, 1989, 1992] referring to the brain's coordinated signaling between redundant, anatomically separated structures that map value-laden categories.) The term *value* therefore condenses aspects of memory, emotions, and motivation. In this sense, it crosses any imagined border or divide between body and mind.

A very similar border-crossing idea of selection is implicit in the Freudian term *cathexis*. As with *value*, the term *cathexis* is also a metaphor implying a certain quantity. For Freud, the quantity was that of a presumed psychic energy that could be attached to a thought, a part of the body, or an object in the world. Cathexis crosses the body / mind boundary, as it unites both memory and embodied desire. When an object is cathected, there is no distinction between mind and body. The term *cathexis* is a neologism invented by Freud's translator James Strachey to render Freud's term

Besetzung, but we are informed that Freud was unhappy
with Strachey's neologism because of his dislike of technical
terms (Laplanche and Pontalis 1973). *Besetzung* is a German
colloquial expression that implies taking something over
and using it in a certain way. It often calls to mind a military
image of capturing and holding some place, which is then
said to be *besetzt,* a metaphor that implies force and quantity
(Ornston 1985). This term first appeared in "The project for
a scientific psychology" (1985). Freud used it to denote elements that were "filled up" with psychic energy; in this context, cathexis was thought of as similar to an electrical
charge that can be applied, in parallel fashion, to neurons,
affects, or ideas. In "The project for a scientific psychology,"
Freud identified a neural system that combined both motive and memory. In this preanalytic publication, Freud
explained motivation not as a drive but as an aspect of
memory. The theoretical importance of Freud's combining
motive and memory was recognized by the neurobiologist
Karl Pribram (Pribram and Gill 1976), as well as the cognitive scientists Don Tucker and Phan Luu (1998), who note
that if memory is linked to motivation, *cathexis* has an adaptive implication, as does the concept of intentionality, where
motive and memory are combined. "The project for a scientific psychology" was written decades before Freud developed what would become his theory of instincts. Had he
continued to combine memory with motivation, his theory
of instincts would have assumed a form that is more conso-
nant with contemporary neuroscience.

Feeling and Adaptation

That feeling and value selection are essential for adaptation
can be shown by the following example. If the amygdala is

bilaterally removed in vervet monkeys, they can survive in captivity but not in the wild. "Returned to nature, it [the monkey] cannot maintain itself and soon dies. The reason is poignant: the monkey ostracizes itself from the group of monkeys in which it was a part. Indeed, it exhausts itself evading its peers. It seems to be constantly anxious and depressed. *The amygdalectomized monkey can no longer distinguish between friendly and unfriendly gestures on the part of other monkeys, and perceives all approaches as a threat"* (cited by Nauta and Feirtag 1986). Feelings can no longer function as markers for values, so the monkey is unable to interpret social signals. This dissociation of feeling from cognition is reminiscent of a human patient suffering from Capgras' syndrome.

Antonio Damasio (1994) described a similar psychological outcome in a man who suffered extensive damage to his right ventromedial cortex, which receives inputs from the limbic system (see also Nauta and Feirtag 1986). The intellect of Damasio's patient was intact, but he showed an extensive affective flattening, and like the vervet monkey, he seemed to lack the capacity to make judgments and therefore could not make decisions. The frontal-lobe area of his brain was dissociated from his emotions. His memory and intelligence were intact, but as he was not guided by feelings, in judging future expectations he made disastrous financial decisions, in striking contrast to his previously sound judgment. In everyday life he could not establish priorities. There was no "loading of the dice." He could not decide what to do next, what clothing to wear, what food to eat. Without awareness of his feelings, he could not anticipate the future, and therefore could not make decisions. He could not distinguish or differentiate between alternative actions. His emotional blindness eliminated his ability to make choices. His emotional mechanism for determining value was inoperative.

Transcendent Values and the Self

In chapter 5, I described Panksepp's and Damasio's concept of a protoself. They proposed that the limbic system functions as a monitor of the individual's holistic emotional states. In this sense the limbic system is analogous to an unconscious protoself, for the self can be thought of as a system that maintains a psychological cohesion analogous to a physiological homeostasis. The selection of values at the level of the protoself does not require consciousness. This same limbic system that monitors emotions, signaling the individual's holistic homeostatic needs, at a higher level, provides the values that select for the needs of the psychological self.

Values that express the needs of the individual as a whole can be described as transcendent. This transformation of biological values into psychological values would be impossible without metaphor and language. What I am suggesting is that the limbic system, responsive to the individual's homeostatic needs *as a whole,* has an analogue in the need for coherence and the transcendent values that characterize the person, the social self. However, the analogy to physiological homeostasis breaks down, as transcendent values associated with personhood do not necessarily serve self-preservation. As William James observed, it is sometimes in the interest of a particular self not to survive (Myers 1986).

The actualization of the self, in Western culture, is thought to be the highest transcendent value. It takes precedence over the individual's need to survive. An individual may sacrifice his life for a belief. Self-destruction, for some, may be a means of self-actualization. Self-destruction may be an expression of a passionately held belief, the altruistic sacrifice of the self for a "higher" goal.[4] Common sense and folk psychology have maintained that pleasure and pain are also examples of such transcendent goals of the self. If self-actualization is the highest transcendent value in Western culture, can we continue to believe that a calculus of pleasure and pain regulates and directs our lives?

Thomas Aquinas believed that pleasure and pain regulated the lives of animals, but not of men. He said, "Sense appetites takes two different forms: one pleasure-seeking and the other aggressive. The former drives animals to pursue what pleases their senses and avoid what hurts them. What animals fight about is their pleasures: food and sex. [In man] reason can control such emotions" (Aquinas 1264, p. 125).

At the level of pure sensation, we may automatically respond to pleasure and pain as do other animals. We avoid physical pain, as do other animals, and we are not unique in our seeking of sensuous pleasures. That other species seek sensuous pleasure is probably more widespread than we have recognized. It has been suggested that even some fish "enjoy" being tickled. Panksepp and Burgdorf (2000) believe that the high pitched chirping sounds that rats emit when tickled are possibly an indication of laughter. That animals experience pleasure can be inferred from the fact that when given the opportunity, animals fitted with electrodes will voluntarily self-administer electricity into their brains (Panksepp 1998a). They in effect stimulate themselves. Pleasure centers in the brain have been identified in the lateral hypothalamus. This suggests that there is an evolutionary continuity between ourselves and other species regarding "pleasure" centers in the brain. However, if we place pure sensation to one side, there is a sharp discontinuity between ourselves and other species in our capacity to elaborate and interpret the experience of pleasure and pain.[5] Pleasure and pain can be pure sensations, but in accordance with the semiotics of feeling, which I discussed in the previous chapter, pure sensations are immediately transformed by interpretation into feelings, feelings which are selected by the self. Ultimately, it is the self that selects what is pleasurable and painful. As Jerome Kagan observed, "No single biological state defines pleasure because it is finally a judgment" (1998, p. 152).

The experience of pleasure and pain is highly individualized and idiosyncratic and cannot be separated from the context of one's life history. This was known to Spinoza. He said, "Each affect of each individual differs from the affect of another as much as the essence of the one from the essence of the other" (Spinoza 1675, p. 185). If we translate Spinoza's "essence" into the modern concept of self, pleasure and pain, apart from raw sensations, are not universal biological regulatory principles, but are instead interpretations dependent on the self.

Ironically, Freud, who created psychoanalysis as a method for interpreting the experience of the individual, viewed human pleasure and pain as an impersonal psychophysical process, a process that could be explained by the distribution of energy within the mental apparatus. He continued to be influenced by an idea he first formulated in "The project for a scientific psychology" (1895): that pleasure results when the psychic apparatus is relieved of a certain quantity of energy. Here Freud, as he admits (1920), borrowed Gustav Fechner's idea that the nervous system attempts to stabilize itself by reducing the quantity of excitement. Freud's "pleasure principle," we know, was superseded by the death instinct,[6] which went "beyond it," but in both instances Freud sought explanations in universal principles. In this he was expressing a late-nineteenth-century ideal of science.

One promising line of investigation, which accords well with introspection, is the idea that pleasure exists more in expectancy and anticipation than it does in the act of consummation. Animal experiments have shown that the pleasure centers of the brains of monkeys are activated more by expectation then by reward (Panksepp 1998a). I am reminded here of Oscar Wilde's aphorism: "In this world there are only two tragedies. One is not getting what one wants, and the other is getting it."

Feeling and Potential Meaning

Psychoanalysts believe, beyond any shadow of a doubt, that the unconscious mind contains potential meaning. This may be one of the clearest areas of disagreement between psychoanalysis and cognitive psychologists. Psychoanalysis and cognitive scientists believe that the greater part of memory is unconscious, but most cognitive scientists and neurobiologists consider implicit (unconscious) memory to be a form of procedural memory, the memory of motor acts or motor routines, memories that are not in themselves meaningful, as they are not charged with the potentiality to evoke feelings. The belief that the unconscious mind consists of procedural memory will influence one's definition of what is "mental." Many cognitive scientists equate the mental with consciousness. This position is supported by a long tradition that included William James, who also believed that the term *mental* should be reserved for only what is conscious, what can be experienced. What one denotes by the term *mental* is somewhat arbitrary, but to deny the existence of a potentially meaningful unconscious would result in a markedly truncated and distorted view of human nature. If one acknowledges that unconscious memory includes the emotions, one must recognize that the unconscious contains *potential* meaning that determines how we feel, how we act, and how we interpret the world. (I will discuss this subject further in chapter 11.)

I would suggest that the idea of *unconscious intentionality,* which attributes potential meaning to the unconscious mind, can serve as a bridging concept between psychoanalysis, cognitive science, and neurobiology. Although this is not a term used by psychoanalysts, psychoanalysts assume that unconscious intentionality is a determining force, below the surface, that shapes human relationships. Walter Freeman (1999a, 1999b) describes unconscious intentionality as a preafference, a process that precedes both sensation and perception. He emphasizes a fact of life that I would underline: *each individual has idiosyncratic expectations of the world.* Each of our actions in the world can be thought of as a trial action, an experiment based on probabilistic expectations derived from prior experience. On the basis of these prior expectations we probe the world for meaning. Psychoanalysts are very familiar with this fact. Unconscious, probabilistic expectations are a familiar aspect of the psychoanalytic relationship and perhaps of all human relationships as well. The patient's conscious intention regarding the analyst may appear to be directed towards the future but is unconsciously designed to alter the past. The patient's attempt to disconfirm their "pathogenic beliefs" by trial action is considered central to the therapeutic action of psychoanalysis by some investigators (Weiss and Sampson 1986). Some patients will implicitly demonstrate by their actions in their relationship with the analyst: "I will attempt to recreate the past, and you must prove to me that it isn't so."

A Note on "Working Through"

The psychoanalytic concept of *working through* is based on the assumption that the unconscious mind is the source of potential meaning. Freud believed that if a patient, because of repression, does not remember, he may instead "act out" the content of the repressed memory. Action prompted by unconscious memory was thought by Freud to be an equivalent of the memory itself. He described this in the paper "Remembering, repeating, and working through" (Freud 1914). The concept of *working through,* although originally descriptive of an aspect of the psychoanalytic process, extends to ordinary life as well. *When experiences remain unassimilated, we may try repeatedly to complete the action by finding substitutes in metaphoric equivalents.* This is evident in aesthetic experiences.

We know that works of art, especially visual art and music, can function as wordless metaphors and be used as a medium for working through. Those artists whose creations evoke very intense feelings are most likely to provide a means for working through. One example would the paintings of the abstract expressionist Mark Rothko. Hovering, rectangular areas of color that appear to be luminously suspended characterize his work. Most commentators agree that these rectangles of color are wordless metaphors that signify feelings. The feelings most commonly identified are those of loneliness and solitude. The feelings generated by Rothko's art have been interpreted as an expression of his own unassimilated experiences. In a biography of Rothko, James Breslin (1993) suggested that Rothko painted a deficiency, an absence, a great vacuum at the center of his being. Breslin further suggested (1993, p. 280) that Rothko produced paintings that, through their interactions with the viewer, recreate the reciprocities and tensions of an early mother/child relationship. Breslin further noted, "It is as if the painting were static or dead—until brought to life by the physical presence of a viewer" (1993, p. 277). The projection of the feelings of loneliness and solitude combined with the tensions of an early mother/child relationship evokes in some viewers, as Breslin suggests, a sense of absence in the presence of the other. For those viewers who have experienced an affective deadness in their own mothers, Rothko's wordless metaphors will find a powerful resonance.

As a parenthetical note, in an obituary notice of the death of James Breslin, the author of Rothko's biography, it was reported that Breslin, who was a professor of English and not an art historian, changed his career when he made an immediate emotional connection to Rothko's paintings (*New York Times*, Jan. 15, 1996). This occurred when he was depressed following the breakup of his first marriage. Rothko's paintings, he said, "create an empathic space in which to confront emptiness and loss; they create an environment for mourning." *We select objects in current time that will provide the meaning that will enable us to alter the experiences of the past.* We invest those objects with feeling when we perceive a metaphoric correspondence between present experiences and unconscious memory.

Communicating Feeling

In the previous section, where I discussed feelings, values, and the self, I omitted a description of feeling as communication. The self is not isolated. Feelings are in the service of two different functional systems. This means that we need two conceptual languages that parallel these very different functions: one pertaining to individual psychology and feelings as internal perceptions, and the other describing feelings as communication. In psychoanalysis, referring to a one-person and two-person psychology has recognized this distinction. I discussed some of these issues in my book *Psychoanalysis in a New Context* (Modell 1984). There I argued that we need to preserve the language of an individual psychology as well as to promote the yet-to-be-realized language of intersubjectivity.

We all recognize that one may express feelings that are the opposite of what is intended. Hostility may disguise love, and love may mask hatred. Psychoanalysts also know that both conscious feelings and unconscious emotions are contagious, as they evoke mirror reactions in the other person. This is most noticeable in the phenomenon of projective identification, as I discussed in chapter 6. In such cases those feelings that are communicated unconsciously are saturated with highly specified meaning.

Some patients who are severely estranged from their feelings need to be taught to identify what they are feeling and to recognize precisely what it is that they are communicating to others. This is a rather strange and somewhat surprising phenomenon, for it means that the analyst is aware of the patient's feeling even though the patient is not. The analyst receives the communication predominately by means of the patient's tone of voice, and is able to identify anxiety, love, anger, and so forth, and then report this back to the patient.

In this unconscious expression of emotion, we share a continuity with other species, as Darwin observed. Charles

Darwin, in his monograph *The Expression of the Emotions in Man and Animals* (1965), described in great detail, in a variety of animals including man, the species-specific bodily and motoric actions and especially facial expressions that communicate a defined emotion, such as anger, grief, or fear. He provided photographs of faces that illustrated these typical emotions and even described his observations of his own baby's smiles and pouts. The use of the facial musculature to display and communicate specific feelings appears to be an early acquisition in both the development of the individual and the evolution of the species. You will recall that emotional attunement between mother and infant is achieved through a gazing dialogue in which the face, especially the eyes, is salient.

Continuing Darwin's observations, modern research investigating the facial expression of emotion has shown that the interpretation of a specific emotion signified by a given facial expression is not, as might be thought, culturally determined, but is instead characteristic of our species as a whole—one of the few indications of a universal human nature. Eckman, Sorenson, et al. (1969) showed culturally neutral photographs illustrating several categories of feelings—happiness, fear, disgust, contempt, anger, surprise, and sadness. These photographs were shown to both literate and preliterate subjects. Their subjects were from the United States, Japan, Brazil, New Guinea, and Borneo. The authors included subjects from preliterate societies to rule out the possibility that there are culturally acquired stereotypes of facial expression from visual sources, such as movies, television, and advertising. Subjects in these different cultures recognized the same emotions when they were shown standard facial photographs.

A more recent study of emotions and feelings using fMRI (cited in chapter 7) presented subjects with Eckman's standardized photographs of facial expressions (Breiter, Etcoff, et al. 1996). They showed subjects fearful, happy, and neutral faces and learned that the amygdala was activated in response to fearful and not neutral faces. But the amygdala also responded to happy faces in contrast to neutral faces. They concluded that the amygdala responded preferentially to emotion but not to a specific emotion. On the other hand, Panksepp (2000) believes that emotions can be differentiated subcortically, but that EEG, which records electrical activity of the cortex, cannot establish this differentiation at this higher level of cortical function.

It is probable, judging from subjects' responses to emotionally expressive faces, that the same neural pathways are activated both by the perception of emotions in other persons and by the experience of that same emotion within the self. If true, this would explain why feelings are contagious. Furthermore, this emotional mirroring would be analogous to the mirroring effect of intentional motor actions that activate "mirror neurons" (see chapter 10). This mirrorlike emotional activation has been suggested as an explanation of our capacity for empathy by the neuroscientist Vittorio Gallese (2001) and psychoanalysts Wolf, Gales, et al. (2001).

Bonding through the Music in the Tone of Voice

Psychopathology can be very instructive when it creates an absence of a function that is normally present. Some years ago I reported my experience with a group of psychoanalytic patients whose speech did not communicate feeling (Modell 1975, 1980, 1984). Their speech had a monotonous flat quality that induced in me a sleepy, disinterested boredom, a state of withdrawal and detachment. It became apparent that the absence of feeling in their speech served a variety of defensive needs. The communication of feeling (within a therapeutic setup) is essentially attachment seeking. Conversely, the noncommunication of feeling is saying, in effect, "I need nothing from you. I can be self-sufficient." When patients fail to communicate feeling, the analyst's empathic imagination cannot operate. This may serve the function of preserving the privacy of the self. One cannot be known if one does not communicate feeling.

Feelings are communicated through alterations in pitch, cadence, and the rhythmicity of speech. The feeling components of speech could be described as musical. Feelings are not communicated when speech tends to be flat and unwavering in pitch and rhythm, and therefore unmusical. What this example teaches us is that variations in the rhythm and pitch of speech, associated with feeling, promotes bonding, and conversely when speech is depleted of its musical elements, distance is created. The psychologist William Benzon (2001) described the relation between musical rhythm and bonding in a variety of cultural contexts. Darwin speculated that singing preceded the evolution of speech and that musical sounds "afforded one of the bases for the development of language" (1872, p. 880).

Many researchers have observed that the rhythmic and musical elements that communicate feeling in speech also contribute to the bonding between mother and infant. Ellen Dissanayake (2000) has summarized this literature that has demonstrated the importance of shared temporal rhythms in promoting bonding between mother and infant. From this it might be inferred that our need for music is deeply entrenched in our body and our earliest intersubjective experiences. The bonding effect of sharing a rhythmic beat, the dialogue of attunement, can be traced to our first relationship and persists to some extent throughout our life. The historian William McNeill, in his book *Keeping Together in Time* (1995), elaborated this point. He noted that group cohesion is maintained by singing together, dancing together, and marching together.[7] This is true of all societies. Dancing together appears to be a primordial function, as it is present in all known cultures, present and past, including the cultures of the Paleolithic era—there are dancing figures in Paleolithic cave paintings.

9   Imagining
       Other Minds

Metaphor relies on what has been experienced before and therefore trans-
forms the strange into the familiar; without metaphor we cannot imagine
what it is to be someone else, we cannot imagine the life of the Other.

Cynthia Ozick

Imagining other minds is the work of novelists, but only
recently has the capacity to imagine other minds been
viewed as an appropriate object of scientific investigation.
Imagining other minds, which is known in cognitive science
as a "theory of mind," received its impetus from two different directions: the comparative psychology of primates and
observations of autistic children. Most autistic children are
missing a capacity to identify with another's intentionality.
They lack what can be described as empathy, or as cognitive
scientists prefer to say, "a theory of mind." This is a defining
characteristic of autism.

Some philosophers, following Descartes, have questioned
whether it is logically possible to know other minds. Descartes believed that it is only the self, one's own mind, that
can be known with certainty; other minds are logically unknowable. Vico, in contrast, believed that other minds could

be known directly. For Vico, knowledge of other minds is a superior form of knowledge. He maintained that our knowledge of other minds is privileged, in the sense that we can imaginatively enter into other minds and understand the works of human creation in a way that is not possible with regard to inanimate or other natural objects. Vico recognized a fundamental distinction between our knowledge of ourselves, which includes knowledge of history and social institutions, of which we are the authors, and knowledge of the natural world, which exists outside of our minds and would remain even if we did not exist. Knowledge of other minds is a form of knowledge that differs from both the third-person perspective of objective science and the introspective or phenomenological perspective.

Psychoanalysts do not question that one can acquire knowledge of others by imaginatively entering into their experience and reconstructing their inner reality. But many neuroscientists would dismiss this form of empathic, dyadic, intersubjective knowledge as unreliable and hence unscientific, since it is not subject to third-person verification. Furthermore, how is one to know that empathic knowledge is not simply a mistaken projection of the observer, what William James (1890) called "the psychologist's fallacy," which he described as "the confusion of his own standpoint with the mental fact about which he is making his report."

Studies of autistic children suggest that our capacity to know other minds is most probably an innate form of knowledge (Baron-Cohen 1999). Our knowledge of other minds may represent a form of cognition that is uniquely human, although, as I shall shortly describe, this claim is controversial. Human infants, in contrast to chimpanzees, demonstrate this cognitive faculty to recognize other minds at approximately nine months of age, although some infant observers, such as Colwyn Trevarthen (1989), claim that infants can have knowledge of others' intentionality as early as three or four months.

Can Nonhuman Primates Attribute Mental Agency to Others?

The psychologist Simon Baron-Cohen, when investigating autism (1999), introduced the term *intentionality detector* as a marker of innate knowledge of other minds. The term *intentionality* in this context refers not simply to goal-directed behavior but more specifically to the attribution of mental processes in the other that are recognized as similar to one's own experience. Baron-Cohen notes that nonhuman primates can be Machiavellian in their social interactions, but this does not demonstrate that they have a theory of other minds, that they are "mind readers." Their Machiavellian actions may be prompted by the contextual perceptions of specific behaviors in the other and is not to be taken as evidence of their being able to detect a complex intentionality in the other. Baron-Cohen concludes that it is unclear whether or not nonhuman primates possess this "higher-order" attribute of intentionality.

The psychologist Michael Tomasello, who has investigated both human infants and chimpanzees, is convinced that a theory of other minds is a uniquely human attribute (1999). He states that chimpanzees lack a theory of mind in the sense that they do not recognize others as mental agents engaged in solving problems. Chimpanzees have no difficulty in detecting the other's (lower-order) intentionality and are capable of making complex social appraisals. However, this represents observations of behavior without the inference that one chimpanzee believes that another possesses *a mind like its own.* For example, it was observed that young chimpanzees made requests of their trainer, regardless of whether the trainer was facing them (Tomasello 1999). This suggests that the chimpanzees could not identify with the trainer's need to see them in order to know what they want. It could be said that chimpanzees are behaviorists and not mentalists, that they don't understand subjectivity.

Metaphor and the "As If"

Michael Tomasello (1999) explains that human infants at around the age of nine months attribute intentionality to other minds because they believe that the other person is "like me." Tomasello believes that at about the age of nine months to one year, human infants experience a sense of sameness or identity between themselves and their caretakers. You will recall that in chapter 5, I described experiments that demonstrate that chimpanzees can recognize themselves in a mirror, whereas monkeys cannot. Chimps and probably some other highly intelligent mammals, such as dolphins, may have a sense of a unique self, but they do not necessarily *identify with the other,* they do not recognize that their own awareness of self is shared by other members of their species, they do not conclude that the other is "like me." I will suggest that the ability to identify oneself with another requires an additional capacity, that of conceptual metaphor.

Tomasello's claim that chimpanzees do not have a theory of mind is disputed, however, by Savage-Rumbaugh, Fields, et al. (2001) and Smuts (2001), who cite numerous instances in which these higher primates do evince a knowledge of the other's complex intentionality. Sue Savage-Rumbaugh believes that chimpanzees show evidence that they have a theory of mind in naturalistic settings but may fail to show evidence in an experimental setup in which they are compared to children with advanced linguistic capacities. She cites as an example that a male chimpanzee will cover his mouth when he cannot stop himself from uttering food barks to deny the knowledge of food from others. Similarly, a male will hide his erection when a more dominant male approaches to hide his interest in the female.

The experience that the other is "like me," we describe as empathy. We know that empathy is based on identification, but it is a *partial* identification. We imagine ourselves into other minds by discovering *items* of similarity. With empathy, the identification is but fleeting and transitory; we feel only "as if" we resemble the other person. Empathy involves a sense of similarity while maintaining a sense of difference. To experience the simultaneity of similarity and difference requires the acceptance of paradox, which in turn rests on the cognitive capacity for metaphor. I believe that the play of similarity and difference that makes transitory or partial identification possible is a metaphoric process. I will claim that *our cognitive capacity to empathically know other minds relies on an unimpaired faculty for metaphoric thought.*

Psychopathology demonstrates that those individuals whose capacity for metaphor has become degraded or impaired cannot experience the play of similarity and difference when they identify with the other. What I have observed as a clinician is that identification in such cases is not partial or transitory but absolute and total. There is no sense of the "as if." In such cases, to feel identified with the other is viewed as hazardous, as one may fear the possibility of becoming swallowed up in the other and losing one's sense of self. For example, a female patient who had a history of severe trauma, when she identified with her mother, believed not that she was *like* her mother but that she *was* her mother. Accordingly, the patient felt an inability to empathize with her mother and to see her as a separate person with her own needs and desires. This patient was not able to imaginatively enter into her mother's mind.[1]

Identifying with the other rests on a paradox—that one is similar to the other and yet one remains oneself. *One must be able to accept the paradox of something that both is and is not.* In turn, the acceptance of paradox assumes a capacity for metaphor—a cognitive facility that allows for the play of similarity and difference. Patients who have an impaired sense of metaphor may experience the constructions of transference in psychoanalytic treatment as frighteningly absolute. If such a patient perceives me to be like her mother, she may be unable to recognize that my personality cannot be identical to that of her mother. This may lead to what has been called a transference psychosis.

When metaphors become foreclosed as a response to trauma, such impairments can be circumscribed and limited to metonymic associations to the original trauma. In other instances, as when individuals are exposed to a massively unsafe environment, they may also suffer a global loss of metaphoric capacity that may prove to be permanent. Those who survived the Holocaust, as I noted earlier, live in a world that is beyond metaphor. This loss of the metaphoric capacity may extend to children of survivors through a form of cultural transmission. This loss of the sense of safety appears to have been communicated from the inner world of the parent to the inner world of the child. How this process occurs is not at all clear. What characteristically develops can be described as a primary identification with the parent's experience. Again, there is an inability to accept the paradox of similarity and difference. The parent's memories and the parent's guilt of surviving become the child's own guilt and memories. Instead of the play of sameness and difference that is part of the empathic imagination, the child experiences a total identification with his parent. For example, one child of a survivor, a college student, withdrew and hid from all social contacts (reported in Bergmann and Jucovy 1982). Her father had escaped being murdered by the Nazis by going into hiding. This young woman was not simply behaving like her father when she withdrew from social contacts; she *was* her father in hiding.

The Loss of Empathy in Autism

The previous example indicates how metaphor can be degraded as a consequence of traumatic experiences. The loss of the "as if" reflects an impairment of the imagination, as imagination requires metaphor. Simon Baron-Cohen (1999) has presented studies that demonstrate that the major deficit in autistic individuals consists of what he called "mind blindness"—the inability to identify with the other. This deficit appears to be innate. Baron-Cohen reports the following experiment. Normal children around the age of three or four are presented with the following visual scenario: Sally places her marble in a basket and then leaves the room. Ann enters the room and then transfers Sally's marble to a different location. The children are asked, "Where will Sally look for her marble?" The usual response of normal children is that Sally will look for the marble were she left it, in the basket. Only a small minority of children with autism gave the response that Sally would look where the marble really was. It was clear that most autistic children could not identify with Sally, could not imagine what was going on in Sally's mind. To identify with Sally, one must be able to accept the "as if," the paradox that one can think like Sally and yet not be Sally.

Autistic and normal children were shown a sponge that was painted to look like a rock, made to look "as if" it were a rock. They were then asked, "What does this look like?" and "What is it really?" Normal children between the ages of four and six could say that the object looks like a rock but that it really is a sponge. Most autistic children could not do so. When shown a stone that looked like an egg, normal children would say, "That looks like an egg, but it really is a stone." Autistic children would say, "It really is an egg" (Baron-Cohen 1999). I would interpret this experiment as further evidence of the loss of metaphoric capacity in autistic children. To reiterate, the acceptance in imagination that something "both is and is not" requires the capacity for metaphoric thought, and the absence of this cognitive capacity helps to explain the inability of autistic children to empathize.

Oliver Sacks (1995) presented a remarkable portrait of an autistic adult, the gifted engineer and professor of animal husbandry Temple Grandin. He described her inability to empathize or imagine other minds. Temple could not understand dissembling and pretense and could never quite understand other people's responses to her. When she was younger, she was hardly able to interpret even the simplest expressions of emotion. As a child, she could not enter into imaginative play. Literature that depicted other minds bewildered her. She was confused, she said, by Romeo and Juliet: "I never knew what they were up to." She could not empathize with the characters or follow the intricate play of motive and intention.

Sacks described an episode in which Temple learned how to make blueprints. She watched how a draftsman did it and then she said, "I appropriated him, drawing and all." She swallowed him whole: she became the draftsman. Again, this total identification with the draftsman lacked the "as if" quality of the empathic imagination.

Some Perspectives on Intersubjectivity

The term *intersubjective* usually refers to the reciprocal effect of one mind upon another. Intersubjectivity refers to the area that extends *between* two minds. Intersubjectivity moves beyond individual psychology, and this creates formidable conceptual problems, as we do not have concepts that help us to analyze events that occur *between* two individuals, constructs that describe the effect of one mind's intentionality upon another. We need a theoretical model that includes both intrapsychic and dyadic events.

Intersubjective communication does not require language. We share with other primates the ability to communicate future intent to other minds by means of emotional signals. In social animals, detecting the probability of the other's future intent and action is predicated on the communication of feeling. Marc Hauser (2000) observed that primates will use different acoustic parameters to convey information about their emotional states. This knowledge of the other's emotional state is essential in maintaining social relationships within a group. Knowledge of the other's intentionality that is obtained through vocalization is not the same as imagining another's mind. A theory of mind assumes a detection of intentionality at a higher level of complexity, such as the ability to recognize that the other has the option of making a variety of choices and can dissemble or lie. Detecting intentionality at this level of complexity, has not been shown in other primates and is lacking in those suffering from autism. Temple Grandin did not know what Romeo and Juliet were up to.

Colwyn Trevarthen (1989), a biologist turned infant researcher, believes that in the human infant an intersubjective relationship, a reciprocal responsitivity, is established
shortly after birth. The mother acts particularly quiet and
soft if the baby is sleeping, calming if the baby acts dis-
tressed, friendly and inviting if the baby is attentive. This
reciprocity of feeling is communicated through eye contact,
speech, and touch. Trevarthen describes this as protoconv-
ersation. He compared this mother-infant interaction to a
musical duet. There is no doubt that the infant senses the
mother's intentionality.

The reciprocity and synchronicity of feeling states between mother and infant has been intensively investigated
by Beebe, Lachman, et al. (1997, 2002).[2] Allan Schore (1994)
has described possible neural correlates of these mother-
infant interactions.

While there are extensive descriptions of the reciprocal
feeling states between mother and infant, as I noted, we
have not yet developed the concepts that would enable us
to describe processes occurring between two separate minds
in terms of events in both individuals. Are there "units" of
intersubjective experience that will help us to conceptualize
our knowledge of other minds? Daniel Stern (1995) has proposed a notion of such an interactive "unit," inferred from
the infant's experience of its mother. Stern proposes that the
infant's intentionality, when directed towards the mother,
leads to intersubjectively aroused feelings that are patterned
and linked to memory within a temporal sequence. For example, Stern imagines a nursing sequence in which the infant awaiting the nipple feels expectation, then arousal,
followed by satiation and sleepy relaxation of tension. The
events and feeling contours follow a kind of "narrative" line
that he calls a *protonarrative envelope.* I would interpret
Stern's concept to mean that the infant's intersubjective ex-

perience of being with the mother forms a memorial cate-gory, an early antecedent of what I call affect categories in the adult. Stern, Bruschweiler-Stern, et al. (1998) later de-scribed the similar concept *of implicit relational knowledge* re-garding intersubjective states in adult psychotherapy.

As the detection of the other's intentionality through the communication of feeling is present in nonhuman primates as well as newborn human infants, it is safe to conclude that this is a more primitive function than our knowledge of the more complex perspectives of other minds. This suggests that in our analysis of intersubjectivity in the adult, we should think of a two-phase process. The first phase is that of selection, what captures our interest and intention. The idea of cathexis, a value-driven selection, is useful here. We know that if feelings are not communicated, it is not possible to be empathic. After a feeling has captured our attention, there is a second phase of interpretation in which the self is the point of reference. One then imaginatively feels oneself into the experience of the other.

Psychoanalysis is preeminently an intersubjective experi-ence for both patient and analyst.[3] One question to be an-swered is: How do shared constructions of reality emerge from two different private worlds? How are meanings mu-tually constructed? The psychoanalyst Thomas Ogden (1994) has coined the term *the analytic third,* a shared, mutu-ally constructed subjectivity that differs from that of either participant. The analytic third is reminiscent of the tech-nique of the "squiggle game" devised by Winnicott (1971) as a technique for interviewing children. Winnicott sponta-neously draws a squiggle, which he invites the child to com-plete. He then responds to the child's drawing, and the game continues—the final product illustrating their shared subjectivities.

The problem of shared subjectivities has been investigated in a very different context, that of literary criticism, where shared subjectivities occur between the author and the reader of the text. The Russian philosopher/linguist Mikhail Bakhtin has called this form of intersubjectivity the "dialogical mode" (Todorov 1984). The reader's subjectivity confronts the subjectivity of the author to create a new form of understanding. It is a process not unlike that of psychoanalysis.

Iris Murdoch, in her essay *The Sovereignty of the Good* (1970), reminds us that there is a moral dimension present when we appraise the mind of another, that to be just we must appraise the other person accurately. Murdoch provides us with the following script. We are asked to imagine a mother-in-law who feels angry toward her daughter-in-law. The mother-in-law sees her daughter-in-law as unpolished and lacking in dignity and refinement; she is brusque and always tiresomely juvenile. Gradually, however, this appraisal alters. The mother-in-law now discovers that her daughter-in-law is not vulgar but refreshingly simple, not undignified but spontaneous, not noisy but gay, not tiresomely juvenile but delightfully youthful, and so forth.

I have taken this account as an illustration that empathy, our knowledge of other minds, is never final. Rather, it is a process that we engage in over time. This is similar to William James' pragmatic concept of truth:[4] that we arrive at truth by means of trial actions over time, that a truth is made "true" by events.[5] This is essentially how a psychoanalyst uses empathic knowledge to arrive at an "objective" appraisal of their patient. That knowledge is never final. This open-mindedness,[6] recognition, and acceptance of individuality does have a moral dimension.

10 Mirror Neurons, Gestures, and the Origins of Metaphor

Mimetic skill rests on the ability to produce conscious self-initiated representational acts that are intentional but not linguistic.

Merlin Donald

In a series of remarkable papers Vittorio Gallese and Giacomo Rizzolatti, Italian investigators from the University of Parma, report their discovery of "mirror" neurons in the premotor cortex of monkeys (Gallese, Fadiga, et al. 1996; Rizzolatti and Arbib 1998; Gallese 2000). Using microelectrodes that recorded from individual neurons, they observed that the same neuron fired both when the monkey grasped an object, such as a raisin, and when a human or another monkey performed the same specific action. Mirror neurons respond only to intentional motor actions. This is the first evidence that there is an area in the motor cortex that can respond specifically and only to goal-directed, relational actions.

"Relational" Mirror Neurons and the Concept of Representation

When mirror neurons are activated, there is a very tight, precise correspondence between a specific motor action and neuron firing. For example, if a neuron responded to an object held between the fingers, it would not respond to the same object held by tweezers. Self-initiated actions and the individual's perception of the identical action performed by another evoke the same neural response. So it can be said that the *monkey's brain (and ours as well) is intrinsically relational.* Noninvasive techniques such as fMRI and PET scans have confirmed the existence of mirror neurons in humans as well (Gallese, Fadiga, et al. 1996; Rizzolatti and Arbib 1998). It is a reasonable supposition that mirror neurons are found in all primates.

It is important to emphasize that what is activated in mirror neurons is not simply a response to the visual perception of the object, for these neurons fire only when a specific *action* is observed. Seeing the object itself will not cause the neurons to fire. Of particular interest is that the specific area of the monkey's prefrontal cortex area that contains mirror neurons (F5) is thought to be homologous with Broca's area in the human brain, so the relational specificity of motor actions may constitute an analog for what in the human brain evolved into a capacity to imitate the precise sounds of speech. As Rizzolatti and Arbib state, "This observer / execution matching system provides a bridge from doing to communicating" (1998).

Mirror neurons may help to explain the "representation" of motor actions. Throughout this book, I have criticized the idea that representation is logically coded information. The mirroring of self-initiated actions with those identical ac-

tions performed by the other provides an alternative explanation that may help to explain and redefine the concept of
representation. You will recall that Descartes invoked the
idea of representation to explicate the correspondence between the mind and the world, a correspondence that as-
sures a precise fit between the external object and its
representation in the mind. Descartes believed that this correspondence was due to God's benevolence—that he would
not play tricks on his subjects. The concept of representation
was thought by some philosophers and cognitive scientists
to explain the enigma of meaning, that the object "represented" in the mind corresponded to object in the world, as
the one was translated into the other by means of a code
or some form of "mental language" (see chapter 1). That
a representation is some form of symbolic or logical code
remains a central concept for many in the cognitive-science
community. The discovery of mirror neurons suggests that
certain actions may be represented in the mind because they
trigger a neural link between self and other. This representation of the other's action by means of mirror neurons is direct and immediate and does not require any intervening
symbolic code or a mental language, as there is an instanta-
neous mapping from self to other and from other to self.
Mirror neurons support ecological theories of perception in
that there is an innate coupling between the self and the
other: we respond to directly perceived qualities of the
other's intentionality; we do not require coded information.
Gallese (2001) suggests that mirror neurons may be only one
among other matching mechanisms in the brain that provide a neural explanation for intersubjectivity. Yet, as mirror
neurons fire only in response to the performance of specific
intentional acts, mirror neurons cannot explain the mind's

perceptual representation of nonrelational events, such as inanimate objects.

We know that shortly after birth the newborn human infant shows an innate capacity to imitate motor actions. Meltzoff and Moore (1977) have observed that infants between 12 and 21 days of age and even one hour after birth imitate tongue protrusion and other facial and manual gestures. In the case of the one-hour-old infant, who has not yet acquired any visual memory, it is possible that the infant did have a kinesthetic memory as a consequence of having practiced this gesture of tongue protrusion in utero. Mirror neurons may explain this behavior as a result of the visual experience after birth having matched the memory of the earlier intrauterine kinesthetic experience. This explanation may account for apparent innateness of the infant's imitation. Such behavior can be described as an innate form of kinesthetic empathy. Kinesthesia provides a medium for relatedness. We may, therefore, have underestimated the significance of the infant's imitative gestures. Mirror neurons may also explain the observation that rhythmic kinesthetic sensations promote bonding. We know that rhythmic motion such as dancing fosters a sense of relatedness and union. You recall that the historian William McNeill, in his book *Keeping Together in Time* (1995), observes that all human societies, both ancient and modern, bond together by means of dance. Kinesthesia too should be recognized as a medium of communication. We innately reverberate to the movement of the other.

The Origin of Empathic Feelings

In chapter 6, I described projective identification, a phenomenon that is occasionally encountered in psychoanalysis.

When this occurs, specific feelings associated with traumatic past relationships are somehow "placed" in the analyst. This mysterious unconscious communication of feeling is not in any sense mystical or telepathic, as it now might be explained by mirror neurons. Vittorio Gallese, who with Giacomo Rizzolatti was a codiscoverer of mirror neurons, recently reports that the experience of witnessing pinpricks that the experimenter applies to his own finger will stimulate the same neurons as when the subject receives a pinprick (Gallese 2001). The implication is that our brains resonate to the other's feelings in manner similar to how we resonate with the other's intentional actions. Gallese concludes that mirror neurons are not restricted to motor acts, that our brains may contain a range of different mirror-matching neurons. This research suggests that we use our bodies as a template that enables us to feel our way into the other's experience. This supports the contention that the roots of empathy are in the body, and as with projective identification, this process occurs unconsciously.

Metaphoric Gesture and the Coevolution of Language

The discovery of mirror neurons provides a neural explanation for the fact that the other person's bodily movements are mirrored within the self. One "feels" oneself into another person's gestures: gestures are innately communicative. Inasmuch as mirror neurons are found in Broca's area, this provides some support for the speculation that in the evolution of language, gesture was the ancestor of language, that imitative gesture evolved before the appearance of the high-speed, precisely articulate language that is characteristic of our species. Philip Lieberman, an authority on the evolution of language, claimed that rapid, precise vocal communica-

tion was the engine that produced the modern human brain
(1991). He suggested that ancient hominids, who showed
left-brain asymmetry, lacked the vocal apparatus for modern speech. They presumably had the capacity for a more
complex method of communication than nonhuman primates, but a capacity that fell far short of modern speech.
If ancient humans did not have the apparatus for modern
speech, how did they communicate? The use of gesture
would be one obvious explanation.

This speculation that gesture is the precursor of language
is by no means a new idea. You may recall that Vico thought
that initially humans were without language and communicated by means of signs and gestures, and that then metaphor was the primary mode of knowing and understanding
the world. The French philosopher Condillac, who was born
nearly 50 years after Vico, also believed that gesture preceded spoken language (cited by Corballis 1991). So by the
eighteenth century this idea had a certain currency.

The psychologist Merlin Donald, in *Origins of the Modern
Mind* (1991), emphasized the significance of imitative gesture in the evolution of language. He proposed a theory of
the evolution of language in which a "mimetic culture" was
interposed between the culture of nonhuman primates and
homo sapiens. Donald suggested that early hominids, such
as *Homo erectus,* possessed a complex prelinguistic system
of gestural communication that was superior to that of contemporary nonhuman primates. He hypothesized that such
a system was based on communication by means of imitation. Donald further believed, as did Darwin, that such
gestural communication utilized a new cognitive ability.
Darwin wrote, "The mental powers of some early progenitor of man must have been more highly developed than in

any existing ape before even the most imperfect form of speech could come into use" (1872, p. 463). It seems likely to me that this new mental power that Darwin inferred is the capacity for metaphoric thought. A species that had the capacity for forming conceptual and perceptual metaphors would have expanded its ability for thought exponentially, even though its aptitude for spoken language may have been rudimentary. This would be consistent with the idea, central to this book, that thought can exist apart from language. This would also suggest that the origin of metaphor and the origin of language are not a coincidence, but represent a coevolution. Donald's theory of *mimetic culture,* an argument for gradualist theories of the evolution of language, represents an alternative to a Chomskian conception of the sudden appearance of an "innate language-acquisition device." Donald proposes that a mimetic culture may have existed for over a million years and is possibly associated with *Homo erectus,* who appeared about 1.5 million years ago and survived until several hundred thousand years ago. If *Homo erectus* did possess language, Donald hypothesizes, it was not a very efficient language and needed to be supplemented by imitative gestures.

The psychologist David McNeill (1992), who has analyzed the gestures that accompany modern speech, makes an important distinction between *iconic* and *metaphoric* gesture. Iconic gestures are based on similarity, whereas metaphoric gestures can represent abstracts thoughts and the unseen. Iconic gestures, but not metaphoric gestures, can be observed in chimpanzees and other nonhuman primates. An iconic gesture may simply imitate or abbreviate a motor action, such as holding out a hand to beg for food. Such gestures are commonly used as a form of communication in immature chimpanzees (Wrangham, McGrew, et al. 1994). You may recall the iconic gesture of the female howler monkey in estrus, who will form an oval opening with her lips and will rapidly oscillate her tongue in and out and up and down. It is clear to the observer that the function of this gesture is to invite copulation (Sheets-Johnstone 1984).

In Donald's theory of mimetic culture, metaphoric gestures are complex and generative, in that they can be broken down into partial elements and recombined into novel forms. Metaphoric gestures could be used to communicate complex emotional intentional states. If spoken language is absent or inefficient, metaphoric gesture could fill in the gap. I am reminded of the use of gestures on the old silent screen, where the actors conveyed emotions by means of exaggerated facial expressions and bodily movements. Donald suggests that the expression of intentionality through gesture may have enabled our ancestors to *voluntarily* communicate emotional intentions. This ability to voluntarily communicate a complex intentionality distinguishes a mimetic culture from that of nonhuman primates. If voluntary control of the expression of emotion characterizes mimetic culture, this capacity would promote the cohesion of the social group. We know that our voluntary control of emotional expression coexists with an older involuntary limbic system that we share with other primates. This combination of involuntary and voluntary communication may be similar to what Darwin (1965) observed with regard to the smiling response in humans. He contrasted the true or involuntary smile, in which the orbicular muscles of the eyes are contracted, with the voluntary smile. We share with other species the homologue of the involuntary smile, while the intentional smile is uniquely human.[1]

Terrence Deacon, in *The Symbolic Species* (1997), proposed that language did not evolve as a separate modular faculty but that it co-opted preexisting cognitive structures. Language and the brain evolved together. It would be equally true to claim that metaphor and language represent a co-evolution, that language co-opted the preexisting cognitive faculty for metaphor. The evolution of a vocal apparatus that can imitate the precise sounds of others would have utilized the prior existence in the brain of mirror neurons that support precise gestural imitation. This enhanced motor capacity to communicate precisely would then be exponentially enhanced by the acquisition of metaphor.

Metaphoric Gesture in a Ritual Dance

We will never know the form that mimed gestures assumed in Donald's hypothesized mimetic culture of *Homo erectus*. However, we do know something of mimed gesture in contemporary aboriginal cultures, such as the rain dance of Native American Indians. A remarkable account of such a dance was provided by the art critic Aby Warburg (1995), who described the rain dances of Pueblo Indians as they were performed at the end of the nineteenth century. In one such rain dance the dancers held live rattle snakes. The snake is treated as a symbol of lightning because rattle snakes move in zigzag patterns that correspond metaphorically to the zigzag appearance of lightning. In Warburg's description, the dancer hurls the snake with great force onto a sand painting that depicts lightning streaks in the form of serpents. The magic of the dance is thus based on a visual metaphor created by the dancers. Metaphor is mimed. Warburg describes this as "danced causality." Of course, in contrast to Donald's hypothesized "mimetic culture," the context of mimesis in aboriginal culture is that of a highly evolved and sophisticated religious system of thought. While we may no longer believe in "danced causality," we remain open and reactive, as were our ancestors, to the evocative power of the mimetic gestures of the dance. Our response to mimesis is phylogenetically ancient and developmentally innate.

**Experience and the
Mind-Body Problem**

*The development of concepts [in biology] can be as powerful a tool as the
formulation of laws in understanding physical phenomena.*

Ernst Mayr

As William James (1904) famously noted, the word *consciousness* does not stand for an entity, a single thing; it is a *process.* The philosopher D. J. Chalmers (1998) reminds us that there are multiple aspects to consciousness seen as a process: consciousness is not uniform. He proposes that the *experience* of consciousness should be differentiated from the *functions* of consciousness. Chalmers identified experience as *the hard problem.* Although the functions of consciousness can be scientifically investigated and science can uncover the neural correlates of a *function* of consciousness, such as attention, the quality of being and feeling, the felt quality of redness or the experience of the dark, are of a different order. For example, the neural pathways that instantiate the *process* of visual imagination may be identified by means of fMRI. Brain imaging may detect that a specific locality in my visual cortex will light up when I imagine the Washington monument, but fMRI will not be able to differentiate whether I am visualizing the Washington monument or the Mona Lisa. A functional analysis of consciousness is possible, but the instruments of neuroscience—fMRI, EEG, MEG—will not uncover the constituent mechanisms of a particular feeling, image, thought, or sense of being.[1]

Providing a neural explanation of a *particular* experience is not simply the hard problem, but it appears to be an insoluble problem when approached from the third-person perspective of science. Experience, what it means to be and feel, can be known only directly through self-awareness, a first-person perspective. Neuroscience can explain a process, mechanism, or function, but it cannot explain the particular content of an experience. Chalmers has performed a very useful service in differentiating the phenomenology of experience from other aspects of consciousness that can potentially be investigated from a third-person scientific perspective.

In addition to knowledge gained from first-person and third-person perspectives, we also obtain knowledge of other minds, by means of empathy, as I discussed in chapter 9. This dyadic knowledge of other minds can be described as knowledge provided by a second-person perspective.

The majority of neuroscientists, with some exceptions,[2] and most philosophers, apart from Vico, when considering the mind-body problem, omit reference to the second-person perspective, knowledge of the consciousness of the other. Such second-person, intersubjective, relational knowledge does have constraints. For one, it is contingent on what the other person consciously or unconsciously wishes us to know. In addition, relational knowledge can be described as aspectual: we can only know aspects of the other's experience; what another is experiencing cannot be known exhaustively. There is a facet of one's self that is intrinsically private and unknowable. Donald Winnicott wrote, "Although healthy persons communicate and can enjoy communicating, the other factor is equally true, that each individual is an isolate, permanently noncommunicating, permanently unknown, in fact unfound" (1963). (I have discussed this point in greater detail in *The Private Self* [Modell 1993].) But despite these constraints, it would be foolish to deny that we can have knowledge of other minds.

The Mind-Body Problem and Some Explanatory Metaphors

The so-called mind-body problem, how purely neurochemical and electrical processes can be experienced as an image or a desire, has existed ever since Descartes separated the "immaterial, immortal, and indivisible soul" from the material body. Descartes asserted that the rational soul could not in any way be derived from the power of matter (1641, p. 118). Spinoza, on the other hand, assumed that mental phenomena are the subjective aspects of states that can also be described physically (Nagel 1995). No philosopher or scientist today is a substance dualist; no one believes in an immaterial mind. However, Descartes' influence has been so profound that traces of this Cartesian duality persist even among eminent scientists, as this quote from Sir Charles Sherrington indicates: "Mind for anything perception can encompass goes therefore in our spatial world more ghostly than a ghost. Invisible, intangible, it is a thing not even of outline; it is not a 'thing'" (1940, p. 247).

A variety of metaphors have been used to deal with the mind-body problem. Some philosophers, as well as neurobiologists, have employed the metaphor of *emergence* to explain the state transition from physical to mental, how matter becomes mind. I don't know of any metaphors that move in the opposite direction—to explain how mind becomes matter. Neuroscientists are not apt to raise this question, but the philosopher Jaegwon Kim asks, "How is it possible for the mind to exercise its causal powers in a world that is fundamentally physical?" (1998).

Descartes relied not on metaphor but on an anatomical explanation to account for the connection between mind and body. He believed that the body affected the mind through a singular midline anatomical structure, the pineal gland. The pineal itself was a selective motor organ, suspended in a whirl of "animal spirits," dancing and jigging "like a balloon captive above a fire."

Freud, you will recall, used the metaphor of representation to explain the transformation of a sexual instinct into a fantasy. The term *representation* is a political metaphor. A (Freudian) representation could be thought of as an ambassador from the domain of instincts, which, to be understood, had to speak a language recognizable to the mind. Freud had previously searched for border-crossing concepts when he described, in "The project for a scientific psychology," a class of neurons to which he attributed both the functions of memory and motivation. Freud retained the idea of a mind-brain unity when he used the metaphor *Besetzung* (literally, to take possession of), which has been translated as *cathexis.* As I noted in earlier chapters, *cathexis* is a border-crossing metaphor, as it unites both memory and embodied desire. When an object is cathected, there is no implied distinction between mind and body. *Emergence, cathexis,* and *representation* are all bridging metaphors.

Is the Unconscious Mental?

In 1958 the philosopher Herbert Feigl summarized the criteria that can be used for distinguishing the mental from the physical world (see table 11.1).

How we differentiate the mental from the physical has never been a simple matter. It is not something that can be decided by arbitrary criteria. There is no agreement among philosophers and neuroscientists on the definition of *mental*. Many would equate the mental with consciousness, as did William James. But then that would mean that all unconscious processes are nonmental. But the mental has also been linked with intentionality and meaning. Experiential memory is unconscious and is, as I have repeatedly shown, the source of potential meaning. Searle recognizes an unconscious mental state "as one that implies accessibility to consciousness" (1992, p. 152), so for him an unconscious state has the *potential* of becoming mental. If unconscious processes are potentially meaningful, and there is little doubt

Table 11.1
Criteria for distinguishing the mental from the physical

Mental	Physical
Subjective (private)	Objective (public)
Nonspatial	Spatial
Qualitative	Quantitative
Purposive	Mechanical
Mnemic	Nonmnemic (before the discovery of DNA)
Holistic	Atomistic
Emergent	Compositional
Intentional	"Blind," nonintentional

Source: Feigl 1958

that they are, the designation *mental* cannot be restricted to consciousness.

I would select from Feigl's table the terms *emergent* and *intentional* as the most salient characteristics that describe what is mental, although the concept of emergence is not limited to mind, as the term *emergence* was popularized by the geneticist Lloyd Morgan in the context of evolutionary systems. Mayr (1982, 1997) notes that inorganic systems were considered emergent as long ago as 1868. T. H. Huxley observed that the peculiar properties of water, it's "aquosity," could not be deduced from our understanding of the properties of hydrogen and oxygen. The concept of emergence, when applied to biological systems, can be stated simply: new properties emerge at higher levels of integration if they could not have been predicted from knowledge of the lower-level components (Mayr 1982, 1997). From a God's eye view of evolution, consciousness can be viewed as such an emergent property.

Eliminating mind from the unconscious may appeal to those who wish to achieve clarity through simplification. This was the strategy of behaviorism, which eliminated mind altogether. While most neurobiologists and cognitive scientists recognize the importance of unconscious procedural memory, the memory of motor routines is devoid of personal or autobiographical significance, that is to say, procedural memory is devoid of meaning. Motor routines can be placed in the service of intentional acts, but in themselves they cannot be described as intentional. If the unconscious were limited to procedural memory, one could construe the unconscious as only an impersonal neurophysiological process. Nor are motor routines emergent, in the sense of the emergence of a system that is unpredictable in its complexity. But, in contrast to procedural memory, the expression of unconscious emotional memory is emergent in its unpredictability and complexity. This book is predicated on the assumption that the unconscious contains *potential* meaning. To believe otherwise would deny the existence of an unconscious metaphoric process and the existence of unconscious intentionality.

In 1915b, Freud, responding to the question of whether the unconscious is mental, observed that if the unconscious is not seen as an aspect of mind, this would *deny the psychological continuity between unconscious and conscious events,* for which there is overwhelming evidence. Freud's argument is still relevant. For if one grants that unconscious memory is potentially meaningful, it makes no sense to disrupt the continuity between what is unconscious and what is conscious.

Emergence, Grounding, and the Problem of Naive Reductionism

The concept of emergence and the associated idea of grounding have also been applied to the relation between sciences, in the sense that new properties emerge at higher levels of integration. For example, human psychology represents a "higher" level of integration, which in turn is "grounded" in neurobiology. But this does not in any way suggest that a human psychology can be "reduced" to neurobiology. We can define *grounding* as an explanation derived from a discipline other than the one that is the initial source of observation, an explanation derived from concepts that are external to one's own field of investigation. As an example, psychology is "grounded" in evolutionary theory. The metaphor of *grounding* suggests that one discipline is more fundamental, which then places the emergent discipline in a dependent relationship and raises the problem and dangers of naive reductionism.

Physics, by restricting its subject matter, is the only science that is independent and sufficient into itself,[3] in the sense that physics provides a more "fundamental" explanation to other sciences.[4] But reduction has its problems when we move from the mind to the brain. When scientists uncover the "neural correlates" of a psychological event, this does not imply that a description of the neural correlates "explains" the psychological event. A neural correlate, as the term implies, simply *correlates* a neural and psychological event; a neural correlate is not an explanation.[5] Nor does the discovery of a neural correlate of a psychological occurrence imply an identity or isomorphism between a discrete event in the brain and its psychological expression. To believe in such an identity would represent a naive form of reductionism. Contemporary philosophers of mind such as Searle (1992), Nagel (1986), Putnam (1999), and Kim (1998) are all materialists, and each in his own way seeks a different solution to this problem of naive reductionism. They all criticize any isomorphic correspondence between the physical and mental, which in philosophy is called *identity theory*.

An example of naive reductionism can be seen in the idea of *consilience*, a vision of a unified science proposed by the entomologist Edward O. Wilson (1998). The transition from the physical to the mental and from biology to culture appears to Wilson not to offer any conceptual resistance. He believes that biology and social science can be unified, and he describes what he calls "basic units" of culture, presumably analogous to the fundamental elements of natural science.

In contemporary philosophy of mind the term *supervenience* is a concept that is similar to the idea of *emergence*.

The idea is that the mental "supervenes" upon the physical, the mental is "realized" by the physical, the mental "emerges" from (but is not identical to) the physical (Kim 1998). As applied to the relationship between human psychology and neurobiology, this idea entails that the explanations of human psychology supervene on neurobiology but not fully reducible to neurobiology. But several eminent philosophers such as Putnam, Kim, and Nagel do not believe that supervenience solves the mind-body problem.[6]

Again, a Plea for an Epistemic Pluralism

In chapter 1, I argued for an epistemic pluralism that recognized the dangers that might follow from a perfectionist pursuit of absolute certainty. This striving for certainty may result in oversimplifications that represent a revival of behaviorism. The behaviorists attempted to make psychology "objective" by restricting observation to what is externally visible. As Keijzer (2001) noted, behaviorism ignored what was internally generated, and everything that I would call mind became an intervening variable. Behaviorism was a method that effectively ignored everything in between input and output, which is the mind itself.

John Watson, the father of behaviorism, described its credo in 1913 as follows:

Psychology, as the behaviorist views it, is a purely experimental brand of natural science. Its experimental goal is the prediction and control of behavior. Introspection forms no essential part of its methods, nor is the scientific value of its data dependent upon the readings with which they lend themselves to interpretation in terms of consciousness. The behaviorist, in his efforts to get a unitary scheme of animal responses, recognizes no dividing line between men and brutes. (Cited by Corballis 1991)

Sir Charles Sherrington, in *Man on His Nature* (1940), describes mind as "all that counts in life": "desire, zest, truth, love, knowledge, 'values,' and seeking metaphor to eke out expression." This description of mind includes all that behaviorism leaves out.

A canon of scientific method is that one starts with the phenomenon. If the phenomenon is consciousness, I must repeat: one cannot exclude from a scientific explanation of consciousness either subjective, first-person experience or the relational experience of two conscious minds in interaction. Indeed, the neuroscientist cannot know of the existence of consciousness without reference to his or her own experience. As the philosopher Thomas Nagel says, "We cannot forget about those subjective starting points indefinitely." Nagel has argued in his essay "Mind" (1986) that it is misguided to believe that a particular (scientific) conception of objective reality is exhaustive. He states, "The first stage of objectification of the mental is for each of us to be able to grasp the idea of all human perspectives, including one's own, without depriving them of their character as perspectives. It is the analog for minds of the centerless conception of space for physical objects, in which no point has a privileged position. To insist on trying to explain the mind in terms of concepts and theories that have been devised exclusively to explain nonmental phenomena is both intellectually backward and scientifically suicidal."

The late neuroscientist Francisco Varela (Varela and Shear 1999, Varela 1999) and the psychologist Max Velmans (2000) have emphasized the importance of including phenomenology in a pluralistic epistemology of consciousness. Varela termed such a pluralistic perspective *neurophenomenology*. Varela integrated the phenomenology of the present moment of experience with global brain events described by nonlinear dynamic systems. His is admittedly a tentative offering, but its significance lies in its attempt to initiate a pluralistic epistemology. I believe that there is a growing awareness within the cognitive-science community that phenomenology cannot be omitted from a scientific account of consciousness. The importance of a two-person perspective has recently been noted in that an entire issue of the *Journal of Consciousness Studies* (Thompson 2001) has been devoted to an investigation of consciousness from the perspective of intersubjective relationships.

As a final observation on the mind-body problem I turn again to the moderating voice of the philosopher Thomas Nagel (1998). The mind-body problem is, in his opinion, still unsolved. What is required for its solution, he suggests, is a radical revision in our concept of mind, a radical alteration in how we conceptualize mind. It requires an unimagined expansion of the concept of mind that would simultaneously include neural events. Mental states have a "tripartite essence—phenomenological, functional, and physiological." It is an illusion to conceive of these aspects separately.

Notes

Chapter 1

1. That is the subtitle of Edelman and Tononi's *The Universe of Consciousness* (2000).

2. For a detailed description of the history of the disembodiment of meaning within philosophy, see Lakoff and Johnson 1999.

3. For example, the influential nineteenth-century philosopher Frege (1848–1925) distinguished "ideas" and "senses." The latter was believed to have nothing to do with human psychology and to be free of subjective meaning. If one believes that "senses" are outside of psychology, it is possible to believe in an isomorphic correspondence between the mind and the world.

4. Cited by Richard Lewontin (2001, p. 383).

5. Searle (1997) famously introduced the Chinese-room thought experiment. Searle imagines himself locked in a room where he is given instructions in English for manipulating Chinese symbols. Following an algorithmic instruction, Searle answers the original questions in English in Chinese without having any knowledge of the Chinese language. His point is that the operations of a computer may be analogous to following the rules of syntax, but syntactical rules do not produce meaning, whereas the mind does.

6. For a detailed discussion of Descartes' influence upon cognitive science, see Lakoff and Johnson (1999).

7. Eccles maintained the Cartesian split between brain and mind by postulating the existence of millions of mental "psychons" that are linked to the

brain's dendrons. "Psychons" are thus postulated mental units that are symmetrical to and ontologically separate from the brain's dendrons.

8. Keijzer states, "The organism does not represent its environment in a static and well-defined way. Instead there is a continuous mutual influence which is too complex to allow description in the impoverished language of representations" (2001, p. 179).

9. Koch and Laurent state, "The dendritic trees in mollusks and insects are as profusely branched and varied as in a primate's brain. The dynamics of firing of a lobster's neurons are at least as rich as those in the mammalian thalamus or neocortex. And neither can be reduced to canonical integrate-and-fire models. Exquisite molecular machines endow neurons with complex nonlinear dynamical properties regardless of the animal's size or evolutionary lineage. Moreover these properties are not static, but adaptively tunable" (1999).

10. Edelman's view of the brain is radically different. He has steadfastly opposed, in all of his publications, informational and computational assumptions regarding the neurodynamics of the brain.

11. Freeman's view of the brain in *How Brains Make Up Their Minds* (1999b) includes the uncertainty of nonlinear dynamical systems.

12. Lakoff and Johnson in their recent book *Philosophy in the Flesh* (1999) argue against the metaphor of mind as disembodied, formal symbolic language.

13. I refer to information theory as it is customarily construed: as a discrete symbolic code. Kelso suggests an alternative view: that pattern dynamics is also informational (1999, p. 408). Information theory may then have relevance regarding events *within* the brain but not as a means of finding a correspondence between events in the world and events in the brain.

14. For a criticism of mentalese, see Edelman 1992.

15. Ramachandran and Blakeslee (1998) describe an experiment with a patient who had the illusion that a hand was telescoped to the end of his phantom limb. Ramachandran placed a coffee cup in front of the patient and asked him to grab it with his phantom limb. "Just as he said he was reaching out, I yanked away the cup. 'Ow!' he yelled. 'Don't do that! I had just got my fingers around the cup handle when you pulled it. It really hurts!'"

16. The psychologist Jerome Bruner has observed that as the child enters language, there are biological constraints that select certain classes of mean-

ing to which human beings are innately tuned and for which they actively search. For this reason he has used the expression *the biology of meaning*. He is, as far as I know, the first to introduce this term.

17. Freud here was arguing for the "mentalization" of the unconscious, as opposed to the idea that the unconscious is only a neurophysiological process and therefore cannot be called "mental." This issue today remains unclear and controversial as there is no satisfactory solution to the mind/body problem: how does a physical process in the brain become subjective experience? This mind/body problem will be discussed in chapter 10.

Chapter 2

1. Rycroft (1996) observed that in Darwin's text one reads "art of poetry," which he thinks was a mistranslation of the German "Art," meaning "kind."

2. For an extensive discussion of the function of metaphor in mathematical thought, see English 1997.

3. The theory of neuronal group selection (TNGS) can be viewed as an example of a "Darwin machine." Edelman was guided by the assumption that some elements of Darwin's theory of evolution—competitive selection within a large population of unique individuals—are operative in the brain. TNGS is a theory of somatic selection. Somatic selection does not, of course, alter the DNA, though it may do so indirectly by modifying the phenotype—the so-called "Baldwin effect." For a discussion of the Baldwin effect, see Depew 2000.

4. Indeterminism is also implied in the variability of functional interactions between neuronal groups. Tononi and Edelman (Tononi and Edelman 1998, Edelman and Tononi 2000) introduced what they call the *dynamic core hypothesis* as an explanation of the neural correlates of consciousness. Unconscious processes are understood to be outside of the dynamic core. This description of a *functional* interaction, the functional linking of anatomically separate brain structures, avoids the problem of cerebral localization. The hypothesis illustrates "the role of functional interactions among distributed groups of neurons rather than their local properties. The same group of neurons may at times be part of the dynamic core and underlie conscious experience, while at other times it may not be part of it and thus not be involved in unconscious process."

5. Freud's meaning was unfortunately obscured by Strachey's translation of *Nachträglichkeit* as "deferred action."

6. Jerome Kagan (1998) has belittled such explanations as having "the allure of infant determinism."

Chapter 3

1. For a further discussion of Freud's conception of "quality," see Pribram and Gill 1976.

2. This would be consistent with Edelman and Tononi's (2000) dynamic-core hypothesis of the neural correlates of consciousness. However, Edelman and Tononi would not agree that thoughts can be unconscious.

3. If one believes repression to be a universal impersonal mechanism, repression could then be explained as a neurophysiological process. Edelman and Tononi (2000) suggest such a neural correlate of repression. Within their description of the dynamic-core hypothesis of the neural correlate of consciousness, they suggest the possibility of the formation of autonomous "splinter cores" as an explanation for repression.

4. I am intentionally leaving to one side the problem of the veridical nature of unconscious memory, which has become the subject of the "memory wars." For a balanced review of this subject, see Prager 1998.

5. I have been maintaining that individual differences are significant at the level of complexity of the self. However, different brain functions may follow different "rules." Where the function of the brain is not concerned with meaning construction, the complexity of the self is not at issue, and individual differences do not make a difference. An example is the visual perception of objects. Here object perception is a brain function in which the self is not a partner and variations among individuals have little or no significance. Donald Hoffman (1998), a cognitive scientist, has show that brains construct visual images in accordance with specified "rules" and "laws."

6. The sleep researcher J. Allan Hobson (1988), who has used cats in his experiments, has a been in the forefront in the attack on Freud's theory of dreams. This is a quote from the conclusion of a recent review in which Hobson compared his theory of dreams to that of Freud's: "In my opinion the new dream theory is so different from Freud's as to make the use of a word like *revision* a euphemism. Because there is essentially nothing left · of the Freudian hypothesis, what is needed is not a revision but complete

overhaul. Instead, what we see is a tenacious adherence to a faith in the interpretability of dreams using vague and unscientific terms like *metaphor* and *hermeneutics* or, what is worse, we see recourse to the relativistic claim of *narrative truth*. This limits psychoanalysis to a literary exercise with no claim to the scientific legitimacy that Freud dreamed of his 1895 'Project for a Scientific Psychology'." If Solms is correct, Hobson cannot infer anything about human dreams from animal investigations of REM sleep.

7. Lacan was one of the first to identify condensation in dreams as a metaphoric process (Roudinesco 1997). The unconscious metaphoric process that characterizes dreaming has also been described from the standpoint of cognitive linguistics by Lakoff (1993).

8. In describing the dream's day residue, I've made use of the summary in Anzieu 1986.

9. In discussing the relation between metonymy and metaphor in chapter 4, I suggest a synergistic interaction rather than an antagonist interaction.

Chapter 4

1. Castoriadis made the same point when he said, "An image must *hold together*; it brings together 'determinate' elements, presentable elements, and these elements always are found caught up in a certain organization and in a certain order—otherwise, there would be no image, there would simply be chaos" (1997).

2. For a detailed demonstration of this process, see Arnheim 1974.

3. The paradox of the constant flux of the sense of self, which at the same time is both continuous and coherent, was seen by William James as a fundamental enigma. James (1890) asks us to imagine a herd of cattle whose owner recognizes their "brand" as his own. These cattle (thoughts) may go their own way; the herd's unity is only a potential one until the owner arrives. The owner actively provides the coherence that underlies the sense of identity of the herd. But how does the owner impose unity and coherence upon the herd? If consciousness is ever changing, how does one establish a continuity between past and present? James suggests that "title" to the herd (sense of self) is passed on from one owner to the another, or to a succession of others (former selves). The succession of "titles" that James describes may be a function of metaphor. At a neural level, as I noted in Modell 1993, Edelman's concept of reentry may also explain this Jamesian paradox.

4. That libido theory could be recast as metaphoric transformations was also noted by Melnick (1997).

5. I have discussed Freud's concept of beating fantasies in Modell 1997.

Chapter 5

1. Others have proposed theories of a biological self. The psychologist James Gibson, in his *Ecological Approach to Visual Perception* (1986), observed that proprioception may also be the source of a nucleus of the self: "In my view, proprioception can be understood as ego reception, as sensitivity to the self."

2. A point also made by LeDoux (1996).

3. The philosopher John Searle (2000) has also described the self as a system property of consciousness.

4. For discussion of this subject, see Tomasello 1999, p. 323. Tomasello believes that we are the only primate who has a "theory of other minds." This contention is contested by Savage-Rumbaugh, Fields, et al. (2001), who present observations confirming that bonobos do have a theory of other minds.

5. In a nearly identical experiment (without the use of anesthesia), before exposing the infant to the mirror, the mother wipes the human infant's face with a washcloth and covertly marks it with a red spot. The infant is then exposed to the mirror and the observer notes whether or not the infant discovers the red spot.

6. The term *social self* should not suggest that I would emphasize the social origins of the self. For I believe, as I explained in Modell 1993, that to a large measure we "bootstrap ourselves" from within.

7. From a very different perspective, Damasio has attributed the triggering effect that I had claimed for metonymy to "somatic markers," containing the memory of former affective states. He refers to the evocation of these somatic memories that bypass actual bodily arousal as "as if" states (Damasio 1994).

8. Eva Brann (1991) has offered a comprehensive review of philosophical commentary on images and imagination.

9. For further examination of Freud and the imagination, see Castoriadis 1987 and Laplanche and Pontalis 1968.

10. I am indebted to Walter Freeman, who provided these citations from Aristotle's *De Anima*: "As sight is the most highly developed sense, the name *phantasia* (imagination) has been formed from *phaos* (light) because it is not possible to see without light. And because imaginations remain in the organs of sense and resemble sensations, animals in their actions are largely guided by them" (bk. 3, chap. 3, p. 217). "All imagination is either (1) calculative or (2) sensitive. . . . Sensitive imagination is found in all animals, deliberate imagination only in those that are calculative: for whether this or that shall be enacted is already a task requiring calculation. . . . It follows that what acts in this way must be able to make a unity out of several images" (bk. 3, chap. 11, p. 231).

11. Scarry (1999) has observed that the remembered face of a loved one may be pale and lifeless compared to the vivacity of a scene that one was led to imagine in a novel or poem. Scarry may have demonstrated the degree to which individuals differ in their imagining.

Chapter 6

1. James Wood, in a critical review of Scarry's thesis (2000), found it to be not entirely convincing. He correctly observes that the visual is not the only modality used to create scenes in novels. Dostoevsky, for example, does not create visual scenes, yet we retain a vivid impression of character.

2. Others have also noted that Vermeer had an uncanny ability to depict the visual process itself. Sanford Schwartz, in an essay on Vermeer, states, "You feel looking at a picture of his that you are seeing atmosphere itself defining the object of your sight" (2001).

3. Freud (1923b, 1933a) had previously assumed that there is a communication between the patient's unconscious and the unconscious of the analyst and also speculated that unconscious affective communication may have been the original, archaic method of communication between individuals.

4. This is true in ordinary usage as well as in the psychoanalytic use of the term.In Kleinian psychoanalysis, *fantasy* is spelled as "phantasy" to indicate the assumption that "phantasy" underlies all mental processes (Britton 1998). This assumption is in accord with my hypothesis of an unconscious metaphoric process. For Klein, unconscious fantasy is the prime mover of the mind. For further discussion of the Kleinian theory of fantasy, see Spillius 2001.

5. Walter Freeman (1999b) has illustrated the application of nonlinear dynamics to neurophysiological events.

6. Johnson (1987) has provided an excellent account of Kant's ideas on imagination.

7. The philosopher Simon Blackburn, in a recent review (2000), referred to Wittgenstein's criticism of Kant's idea of applying rules to experience as involving an infinite regress of rules.

8. A recent commentary on Kant's philosophy of imagination by the philosopher Rudolf Makkreel (1990) does find a place for personal imagination. Makkreel believes that Kant's theory of the imagination can be seen as hermeneutic in that, he claims, Kant viewed imagination to be fundamentally a form of *interpretation*. If this is so, this would be consistent with my own conception.

Chapter 7

1. I am indebted to Nauta and Feirtag (1986) for providing a very succinct history of this development.

2. Joseph LeDoux (1996), in an otherwise excellent account, attempts to maintain this distinction between emotion and cognition.

3. For an extensive discussion of Freud on sublimation, see Loewald 1988.

4. Walter Freeman (1999b) and the neuropsychologist Nicholas Humphrey (2000b) have revived interest in the old distinction made by facultative psychology between sensation and perception.

5. Nicholas Humphrey (2000a, 2000b) distinguishes sensation and unconscious perception but does so in a very different fashion. I see unconscious perception as a process that interprets sensation, whereas Humphrey attributes sensation to the bodily self yet views perception not as an interpretation but as an impersonal cognitive process.

6. The neurologist Kurt Goldstein (1940, p. 60) described a similar loss of complex mental functions in patients with damage to the cerebral cortex. Their behavior was described as "concrete," but importantly, Goldstein noted that in "abstract" performances, action is determined directly and immediately, not by stimulus configuration, but by "the account of the situation which the individual gives to himself." In other words, the loss of the capacity for abstract thought involves a deficit of interpretation.

7. Peirce thought of interpretation, for which he coined the word *interpretant*, as an infinite regression, for each interpretation is based on another

association. For an excellent description of Peirce's contribution to pragmatism, see Menand 2001.

Chapter 8

1. Marcia Cavell (1993) presents an expanded discussion of the construction of meaning from an "internalist" perspective, a perspective that she essentially rejects. Jerome Bruner (1990) examines the same issue from an "externalist" point of view, arguing for the overriding impact of culture. The effect of culture on categorical thought was illustrated in an article in the *New York Times* (Aug. 8, 2000). The report described the research of the social psychologist Richard Nisbett, who compared Americans to East Asians and found that cultural values will influence the categories of thought. For example, people in Japan, China, and Korea, appear to think more "holistically," paying greater attention to context and relationship, relying more on experienced-based knowledge than abstract logic, and showing more tolerance for contradiction. Westerners are more "analytic" in their thinking, tending to detach objects from their context, to avoid contradiction, and to rely more heavily on formal logic.

2. The many windows of consciousness are depicted in novels in which the novelist portrays the multiple inner voices of the protagonist as they shift effortlessly from past to present. This has been illustrated in the multivoiced internal dialogues of Virginia Woolf's *To the Lighthouse.* These multiple inner voices are discussed in relation to theories of consciousness by Scheff (2000).

3. The psychologist Bernard Baars (1997) has enlarged on James' insight that consciousness is a selecting agency, by introducing the metaphor of a global work space.

4. I have described the function of passionately held beliefs in *The Private Self* (1993).

5. Kagan made a similar point in his essay *Three Seductive Ideas* (1998) when he criticized the application of animal models of pleasure to human beings.

6. Jonathan Lear (2000), in his commentary on Freud's death instinct, describes it as a nonexplanation, an "enigmatic signifier."

7. Walter Freeman (1995, 2000) has also emphasized the social-bonding effect of dance.

Chapter 9

1. Peter Fonagy and Mary Target (1998) have described this process as a failure of mentalization. This inability to imaginatively construct other minds, they believe, is a poor prognostic indicator for psychoanalytic treatment when present in the mother or child.

2. Ellen Dissanayake (2000) has provided a very useful summary of current research on early mother-infant interactions.

3. Intersubjectivity has become the focus of a new "school" of psychoanalysis described as relational psychoanalysis. For an overview, see Mitchell and Aron (1999).

4. William James, in his essay "Pragmatism's conception of truth" (1908), described truth as a process.

5. For an amplification of James on truth and pragmatism, see Putnam 1997.

6. This is a theme developed by Lear (1998).

Chapter 10

1. Damasio (1994) recounts that his mentor Norman Geschwind pointed out that the reason we have difficulty smiling naturally for photographers is that they ask us to control our facial muscles willfully.

Chapter 11

1. Edelman and Tononi 2000 is an example a functional analysis of consciousness. Their "dynamic-core hypothesis" states, "The activity of a group of neurons can contribute directly to conscious experience if it is part of a functional cluster, characterized by strong mutual interactions. To sustain conscious experience, it is essential that this functional cluster be highly differentiated."

2. The late cognitive scientist Franisco Varela and the philosopher Jonathan Shear, in contrast to most of their colleagues, have pleaded for recognition of the importance of this two-person relational perspective in the investigation of consciousness (see Varela and Shear 1999).

3. The British zoologist C. F. A. Pantin, in an underappreciated book *The Relation between the Sciences* (1968), described physics as a "restricted" science as compared to "unrestricted" biology, whose subject matter comprises all that is living.

4. In a recent essay (2001), the Nobel physicist Steven Weinberg examined the ideas of *explanation* and *fundamental* in physics. These terms are by no means self-evident. Explanation needs to be distinguished from description without involving the slippery notion of causality. There is no agreement among physicists on what are fundamental principles and what are accidents.

5. This point is elaborated by the cognitive scientist Antti Revonsuo (2001).

6. For a discussion of supervenience, see Putnam 1999 and Kim 1998. Both of these philosophers reject supervenience as a solution to the mind-brain problem. Thomas Nagel writes, "We have good grounds for believing that the mental supervenes on the physical—i.e., that there is no mental difference without a physical difference. But pure, unexplained supervenience is not a solution but a sign that there is something fundamental we don't know" (1998).

References

Allman, J. M. 1999. *Evolving Brains.* New York: Scientific American Library.

Anzieu, D. 1986. *Freud's Self-Analysis.* Madison, Conn.: International Universities Press.

Aquinas, T. 1264. *Summa Theologiae.* Allen, Texas: Christian Classics.

Aristotle. 1934. *Poetics.* J. M. Dent & Sons.

Aristotle. 1947. *On the Soul.* In *Introduction to Aristotle,* edited by R. McKeon. New York: Random House.

Aristotle. 1986. *De Anima (On the Soul).* London: Penguin.

Arnheim, R. 1974. *Art and Visual Perception.* Berkeley: University of California Press.

Baars, B. J. 1997. *In the Theater of Consciousness.* New York: Oxford University Press.

Baron-Cohen, S. 1999. *Mindblindness.* Cambridge: MIT Press.

Bartlett, F. C. 1932. *Remembering.* Cambridge: Cambridge University Press.

Bateson, G. 1972. *Steps to an Ecology of Mind.* New York: Ballantine Books.

Beebe, B., and F. Lachman. 2002. *Infant Research and Adult Treatment.* Hillsdale, N.J.: Analytic Press.

Beebe, B., F. Lachman, et al. 1997. "Mother-infant interaction structures and presymbolic self and object representations." *Psychoanalytic Dialogues* 7 (2): 133–182.

Benzon, W. 2001. *Beethoven's Anvil.* New York: Basic Books.

Bergmann, M. S., and M. E. Jucovy. 1982. *Generations of the Holocaust.* New York: Columbia University Press.

Berlin, I. 1969. "Vico's concept of knowledge." In *Giambattista Vico,* edited by G. Tagliacozzo and H. V. White. Baltimore: Johns Hopkins University Press.

Berlin, I. 1976. *Vico and Herder.* New York: Viking Press.

Bickerton, D. 1995. *Language and Human Behavior.* Seattle: University of Washington Press.

Bion, W. 1972. *Attention and Interpretation.* New York: Basic Books.

Blackburn, S. 2000. "Professor whatever." *New Republic* 438 (4): 34–40.

Bollas, C. 1987. *The Shadow of the Object.* New York: Columbia University Press.

Borbély, A. A., and G. Tononi, 1998. "The quest for the essence of sleep." *Daedalus* 127 (2).

Bottini, G., R. Corcoran, et al. 1994. "The role of the right hemisphere in the interpretation of figurative aspects of language." *Brain* 117: 1241–1253.

Brann, E. T. H. 1991. *The World of the Imagination.* Lanham, Md.: Rowman and Littlefield.

Braun, A. 1999. "Commentary on Allan Hobson's 'The new neuropsychology of sleep: implications for psychoanalysis'." *Neuro-psychoanalysis* 1 (2): 196–201.

Breiter, H., N. Etcoff, et al. 1996. "Response and habituation of the human amygdala during visual processing of facial expression." *Neuron* 17: 875–887.

Breslin, J. 1993. *Mark Rothko.* Chicago: University of Chicago Press.

Britton, R. 1998. *Belief and Imagination.* London: Routledge.

Bruner, J. 1990. *Acts of Meaning.* Cambridge: Harvard University Press.

Castoriadis, C. 1987. *The Imaginary Institution of Society.* Cambridge: MIT Press.

Castoriadis, C. 1997. *World in Fragments.* Stanford: Stanford University Press.

Cavell, M. 1993. *The Psychoanalytic Mind*. Cambridge: Harvard University Press.

Chalmers, D. 1998. "Facing up to the problem of consciousness." In *Explaining Consciousness: The "Hard Problem,"* edited by J. Shear. Cambridge: MIT Press.

Changeux, J.-P. 1997. *Neuronal Man*. Princeton: Princeton University Press.

Changeux, J.-P., and A. Connes. 1995. *Conversations on Mind, Matter, and Mathematics*. Princeton: Princeton University Press.

Clark, A. 1997. *Being There*. Cambridge: MIT Press.

Coleridge, S. T. 1817. *Biographia Literaria*. Princeton: Princeton University Press.

Corballis, M. C. 1991. *The Lopsided Ape*. New York: Oxford University Press.

Crick, F. 1994. *The Astonishing Hypothesis*. New York: Simon and Schuster.

Crick, F., and C. Koch. 2000. "The unconscious homunculus." *Neuropsychoanalysis* 2 (1): 3–10.

Cytowic, R. E. 1993. *The Man Who Tasted Shapes*. New York: J. P. Putnam's Sons.

Damasio, A. 1994. *Descartes' Error*. New York: G. P. Putnam's Sons.

Damasio, A. 1999. *The Feeling of What Happens*. New York: Harcourt Brace.

Darwin, C. 1872. *The Origin of Species and the Descent of Man*. New York: Modern Library.

Darwin, C. 1965. *The Expression of the Emotions in Man and Animals*. Chicago: University of Chicago Press.

Dawkins, R. 1976. *The Selfish Gene*. New York: Oxford University Press.

Deacon, T. W. 1997. *The Symbolic Species*. New York: W. W. Norton.

Depew, D. 2000. "The Baldwin effect: an archeology." *Cybernetics and Human Knowing* 7 (1): 7–20.

Descartes, R. 1641. *The Philosophical Works of Descartes*. Cambridge: Cambridge University Press.

Deutsch, H. 1926. Occult processes occurring during psychoanalysis. In *Psychoanalysis and the Occult,* edited by G. Devereux. New York: International Universities Press.

Dissanayake, E. 2000. "Antecedents of the temporal arts in early mother-infant interaction." In *The Origins of Music,* edited by N. L. Wallin, B. Merker, and S. Brown. Cambridge: MIT Press.

Donald, M. 1991. *Origins of the Modern Mind.* Cambridge: Harvard University Press.

Eccles, J. C. 1993. "Evolution of complexity of the brain with the emergence of consciousness." In *Rethinking Neural Networks: Quantum Fields and Biological Data,* edited by K. H. Pribram. Hillsdale, N.J.: Lawrence Erlbaum.

Eckman, P., E. R. Sorenson, et al. 1969. "Pan-cultural elements in facial displays of emotion." *Science* 164: 86–88.

Edelman, G. M. 1987. *Neural Darwinism.* New York: Basic Books.

Edelman, G. M. 1989. *The Remembered Present.* New York: Basic Books.

Edelman, G. M. 1992. *Bright Air, Brilliant Fire.* New York: Basic Books.

Edelman, G. M. 1998. "Building a picture of the brain." *Daedalus* 127 (2): 37–70.

Edelman, G. M., and G. Tononi. 2000. *A Universe of Consciousness: How Matter Becomes Imagination.* New York: Basic Books.

Edie, J. M. 1969. "Vico and Existential Philosophy." In *Giambattista Vico,* edited by G. Tagliacozzo and H. V. White. Baltimore: Johns Hopkins University Press.

Emde, R. N. 1983. "The prerepresentational self and its affective core." *Psychoanalytic Study of the Child* 38: 165–192.

Emerson, R. W. 1847. "Nature." In *The Complete Essays of Ralph Waldo Emerson.* New York: Modern Library.

English, L. D. 1997. *Mathematical Reasoning.* Mahwah, N.J.: Lawrence Erlbaum Associates.

Fairbairn, W. R. D. 1952. *Psychoanalytic Studies of the Personality.* London: Tavistock Publications.

Fauconnier, G. 1994. *Mental Spaces.* Cambridge: Cambridge University Press.

Feigl, H. 1958. "The mental and the physical." In *Concepts, Theories, and the Mind-Body Problem,* edited by H. Feigl, M. Scriven, and G. Maxwell. Minneapolis: University of Minnesota Press.

Flanagan, O. 2000. *Dreaming Souls*. New York: Oxford University Press.

Fodor, J. A. 1983. *The Modularity of Mind*. Cambridge: MIT Press.

Fonagy, P., and M. Target. 1998. "Mentalization and the changing aims of child psychoanalysis." *Psychoanalytic Dialogues* 8 (1): 87–114.

Frackowiak, R. S. J., K. J. Friston, et al. 1997. *Human Brain Function*. San Diego: Academic Press.

Frazer, J. G. 1994. *The Golden Bough*. London: Oxford University Press.

Freeman, W. J. 1993. "The emergence of chaotic dynamics as a basis for comprehending intentionality in experimental subjects." *Rethinking Neural Networks: Quantum Fields and Biological Data*, edited by K. H. Pribram. Hillsdale, N.J.: Lawrence Erlbaum Associates.

Freeman, W. J. 1995. *Societies of Brains*. Hillsdale, N.J.: Lawrence Erlbaum.

Freeman, W. J. 1999a. "Consciousness, intentionality, and causality." *Journal of Consciousness Studies* 6 (Nov./Dec.): 143–172.

Freeman, W. J. 1999b. *How Brains Make Up Their Minds*. London: Weidenfeld and Nicholson.

Freeman, W. J. 2000. "A neurobiological role of music in social bonding." In *The Origins of Music*, edited by N. L. Wallin, B. Merker and S. Brown. Cambridge: MIT Press.

Freud, S. 1895. *Project for a Scientific Psychology*. In *The Standard Edition of the Complete Psychological Works of Sigmund Freud*, vol. 1. London: Vintage, 2001.

Freud, S. 1900. *The Interpretation of Dreams*. In *The Standard Edition of the Complete Psychological Works of Sigmund Freud*, vols. 4–5. London: Vintage, 2001.

Freud, S. 1905. *Three Essays in the Theory of Sexuality*. In *The Standard Edition of the Complete Psychological Works of Sigmund Freud*, vol. 7. London: Vintage, 2001.

Freud, S. 1906. "Psychopathic characters on the stage." In *The Standard Edition of the Complete Psychological Works of Sigmund Freud*, vol. 7. London: Vintage, 2001.

Freud, S. 1910. *Leonardo Da Vinci and a Memory of His Childhood*. In *The Standard Edition of the Complete Psychological Works of Sigmund Freud*, vol. 11. London: Vintage, 2001.

Freud, S. 1911. "Formulations on the two principles of mental functioning." In *The Standard Edition of the Complete Psychological Works of Sigmund Freud*, vol. 12. London: Vintage, 2001.

Freud, S. 1914. "Remembering, repeating, and working through." In *The Standard Edition of the Complete Psychological Works of Sigmund Freud*, vol. 12. London: Vintage, 2001.

Freud, S. 1915a. "Repression." In *The Standard Edition of the Complete Psychological Works of Sigmund Freud*, vol. 14. London: Vintage, 2001.

Freud, S. 1915b. "The unconscious." In *The Standard Edition of the Complete Psychological Works of Sigmund Freud*, vol. 14. London: Vintage, 2001.

Freud, S. 1917. "On transformations of instinct as exemplified in anal erotism." In *The Standard Edition of the Complete Psychological Works of Sigmund Freud*, vol. 17. London: Vintage, 2001.

Freud, S. 1920. *Beyond the Pleasure Principle*. In *The Standard Edition of the Complete Psychological Works of Sigmund Freud*, vol. 18. London: Vintage, 2001.

Freud, S. 1923a. *The Ego and the Id*. In *The Standard Edition of the Complete Psychological Works of Sigmund Freud*, vol. 19. London: Vintage, 2001.

Freud, S. 1923b. "Two encyclopaedia articles." In *The Standard Edition of the Complete Psychological Works of Sigmund Freud*, vol. 18. London: Vintage, 2001.

Freud, S. 1925. "A note upon the 'mystic writing pad'." In *The Standard Edition of the Complete Psychological Works of Sigmund Freud*, vol. 19. London: Vintage, 2001.

Freud, S. 1933a. "Dreams and occultism." In *The Standard Edition of the Complete Psychological Works of Sigmund Freud*, vol. 22. London: Vintage, 2001.

Freud, S. 1933b. *New Introductory Lectures*. In *The Standard Edition of the Complete Psychological Works of Sigmund Freud*, vol. 22. London: Vintage, 2001.

Freud, S. 1940. *An Outline of Psychoanalysis*. In *The Standard Edition of the Complete Psychological Works of Sigmund Freud*, vol. 23. London: Vintage, 2001.

Gallese, V. 2000. "The inner sense of action." *Journal of Consciousness Studies* 7 (10): 23–40.

Gallese, V. 2001. "The 'shared manifold' hypothesis." *Journal of Consciousness Studies* 8 (5–7): 33–50.

Gallese, V., L. Fadiga, et al. 1996. "Action recognition in the premotor cortex." *Brain* 119: 593–609.

Gaukroger, S. 1995. *Descartes: An Intellectual Biography.* New York: Oxford University Press.

Gelder, T. van. 1998. "The dynamical hypothesis in cognitive science." *Behavioral and Brain Sciences* 21: 615–655.

Geschwind, N. 1965. "Disconnection syndromes in animals and man." *Brain* 88: 237–294, 585–644.

Gibbs, R. W. 1993. Process and products in making sense of tropes. In *Metaphor and Thought,* edited by A. Ortony. Cambridge: Cambridge University Press.

Gibbs, R. W. 1994. *The Poetics of Mind.* Cambridge: Cambridge University Press.

Gibson, J. J. 1986. *The Ecological Approach to Visual Perception.* Hillsdale, N.J.: Lawrence Erlbaum Associates.

Goldstein, K. 1940. *Human Nature.* Cambridge: Harvard University Press.

Gombrich, E. H. 1960. *Art and Illusion.* New York: Pantheon.

Gould, S. J. 2000. "More things in heaven and earth." In *Alas, Poor Darwin,* edited by H. Rose and S. Rose. New York: Harmony Books.

Graves, R. 1948. *The White Goddess.* New York: Farrar, Straus, and Giroux.

Green, A. 1986. *On Private Madness.* Madison, Conn.: International Universities Press.

Greenberg, T., H. Katz, et al. 1992. "A research-based reconsideration of the psychoanalytic theory of dreaming." *Journal of the American Psychoanalytic Association* 40: 531–550.

Grubrich-Simitis, I. 1984. "From concretism to metaphor: thoughts on some theoretical and technical aspects of the psychoanalytic work with children of Holocaust survivors." *Psychoanalytic Study of the Child* 39: 301–319.

Hadamard, J. 1945. *The Psychology of Invention in the Mathematical Field.* New York: Dover Publications.

Hauser, M. D. 2000. "Primate vocalizations in emotion and thought." In *The Origins of Music,* edited by N. L. Wallin, B. Merker, and S. Brown. Cambridge: MIT Press.

Hobson, J. A. 1988. *The Dreaming Brain.* New York: Basic Books.

Hoffman, D. D. 1998. *Visual Intelligence.* New York: W. W. Norton.

Humphrey, N. 1997. "Commentary on Mark Solms' 'What is consciousness?'" *Journal of the American Psychoanalytic Association* 45: 726–731.

Humphrey, N. 2000a. "How to solve the mind-body problem." *Journal of Consciousness Studies* 7 (4): 5–20.

Humphrey, N. 2000b. "Now you see it, now you don't: commentary on paper by Crick and Koch." *Neuro-psychoanalysis* 2 (1): 14–17.

Isaacs, S. 1948. "The nature and function of fantasy." *International Journal of Psycho-analysis* 29: 73–97.

Jakobson, R. 1995. *On Language.* Cambridge: Harvard University Press.

James, W. 1890. *The Principles of Psychology.* New York: Dover Publications.

James, W. 1904. "Does 'consciousness' exist?" In *The Writings of William James,* edited by J. J. McDermott. Chicago: University of Chicago Press.

James, W. 1908. "Pragmatism's conception of truth." In *The Writings of William James,* edited by J. J. McDermott. Chicago: University of Chicago Press.

Johnson, M. 1987. *The Body in the Mind.* Chicago: University of Chicago Press.

Jones, E. 1953. *The Life and Work of Sigmund Freud.* Vol. 1. New York: Basic Books.

Kagan, J. 1998. *Three Seductive Ideas.* Cambridge: Harvard University Press.

Kant, I. 1787. *Critique of Pure Reason.* New York: St. Martin's Press.

Kaplan, D. M. 1993. "What Is Sublimated in Sublimation?" *Journal of the American Psychoanalytic Association* 41: 549–570.

Keijzer, F. 2001. *Representation and Behavior.* Cambridge: MIT Press.

Kelso, J. A. S. 1999. *Dynamic Patterns.* Cambridge: MIT Press.

Kim, J. 1998. *Mind in a Physical World.* Cambridge: MIT Press.

Kitcher, P. 1992. *Freud's Dream.* Cambridge: MIT Press.

Koch, C., and G. Laurent. 1999. "Complexity and the nervous system." *Science* 284: 96–98.

Koestler, A. 1964. *The Act of Creation*. New York: Macmillan.

Kosslyn, S. M., A. Pacual-Leone, et al. 1999. "The role of area 17 in visual imagery: convergent evidence from PET and rTMS." *Science* 284: 167–170.

Lakoff, G. 1987. *Women, Fire, and Dangerous Things*. Chicago: University of Chicago Press.

Lakoff, G. 1993. "How metaphor structures dreams: the theory of conceptual metaphor applied to dream analysis." *Dreaming* 3: 77–98.

Lakoff, G., and M. Johnson. 1980. *Metaphors We Live By*. Chicago: University of Chicago Press.

Lakoff, G., and M. Johnson. 1999. *Philosophy in the Flesh*. New York: Basic Books.

Langer, S. K. 1967. *Mind: An Essay on Human Feelings*. Vol. 1. Baltimore: Johns Hopkins University Press.

Laplanche, J., and J. B. Pontalis. 1968. "Fantasy and the origins of sexuality." *International Journal of Psychoanalysis* 49: 1–18.

Laplanche, J., and J. B. Pontalis. 1973. "The language of psycho-analysis." New York: W. W. Norton.

Lear, J. 1998. *Open Minded*. Cambridge: Harvard University Press.

Lear, J. 2000. *Happiness, Death, and the Remainder of Life*. Cambridge: Harvard University Press.

LeDoux, J. 1996. *The Emotional Brain*. New York: Simon and Schuster.

Lewontin, R. C. 1985. "Darwin, Mendel, and the mind." *New York Review of Books* 32 (15): 18–23.

Lewontin, R. C. 1991. *Biology as Ideology*. New York: Harper Perennial.

Lewontin, R. C. 2001. "In the beginning was the word." *Science* 291: 1263–1264.

Libet, B. 1999. "Do we have free will?" *Journal of Consciousness Studies* 6 (Aug./Sept.).

Lieberman, P. 1991. *Uniquely Human*. Cambridge: Harvard University Press.

Llinás, R. R. 2001. *I of the Vortex*. Cambridge: MIT Press.

Locke, J. 1689. *An Essay Concerning Human Understanding.* Cleveland: Meridian Books, 1964.

Loewald, H. 1988. *Sublimation.* New Haven: Yale University Press.

Louie, K., and M. Wilson. 2001. "Temporally structured replay of awake hippocampal ensemble activity during rapid eye movement sleep." *Neuron* 29: 145–156.

MacLean, P. D. 1949. "Psychosomatic disease and the 'visceral brain'." *Psychosomatic Medicine* 11: 338–353.

MacLean, P. D. 1990. *The Triune Brain in Evolution.* New York: Plenum Press.

Makkreel, R. 1990. *Imagination and Interpretation in Kant.* Chicago: University of Chicago Press.

Martin, A., J. V. Haxby, et al. 1995. "Discrete cortical regions associated with knowledge of color and knowledge of action." *Science* 270: 9.

Masson, J. M. 1985. *The Complete Letters of Sigmund Freud to Wilhelm Fliess.* Cambridge: Harvard University Press.

Mayr, E. 1982. *The Growth of Biological Thought.* Cambridge: Harvard University Press.

Mayr, E. 1997. *This Is Biology.* Cambridge: Harvard University Press.

McNeill, D. 1992. *Hand and Mind.* Chicago: University of Chicago Press.

McNeill, W. H. 1995. *Keeping Together in Time.* Cambridge: Harvard University Press.

Melnick, B. A. 1997. "Metaphor and the theory of libidinal development." *International Journal of Psychoanalysis* 78 (5): 997–1015.

Meltzoff, A., and M. K. Moore. 1977. "Imitation of facial and manual gestures by human neonates." *Science* 198: 75–78.

Menand, L. 2001. *The Metaphysical Club.* New York: Farrar, Straus, and Giroux.

Merkin, D. 1996. "Person history—unlikely obsession." *New Yorker* (Feb. 26 and Mar. 4): 98–115.

Merleau-Ponty, M. 1962. *Phenomenology of Perception.* London: Routledge.

Mitchell, S. A., and L. Aron. 1999. *Relational Psychoanalysis.* Hillsdale, N.J.: Analytic Press.

Mithin, S. 1996. *The Prehistory of the Mind.* London: Thames and Hudson.

Modell, A. H. 1965. "On having the right to a life: an aspect of the super-ego's development." *International Journal of Psycho-analysis* 46: 323–331.

Modell, A. H. 1975. "A narcissistic defense against affects and the illusion of self-sufficiency." *International Journal of Psychoanalysis* 56: 275–282.

Modell, A. H. 1980. "Affects and their non-communication." *International Journal of Psychoanalysis* 61: 259–267.

Modell, A. H. 1984. *Psychoanalysis in a New Context.* New York: International Universities Press.

Modell, A. H. 1990. *Other Times, Other Realities.* Cambridge: Harvard University Press.

Modell, A. H. 1993. *The Private Self.* Cambridge: Harvard University Press.

Modell, A. H. 1997. "Humiliating fantasies and the pursuit of unpleasure." In *On Freud's "A child is being beaten,"* edited by E. S. Person. New Haven: Yale University Press.

Modell, A. H. 1999. The dead mother syndrome and the reconstruction of trauma. In *The Dead Mother,* edited by G. Kohon. London: Routledge.

Muller, J. 2000. "Hierarchical models in semiotics and psychoanalysis." In *Peirce, Semiotics, and Psychoanalysis,* edited by J. Muller and J. Brent. Baltimore: Johns Hopkins University Press.

Murdoch, I. 1970. *The Sovereignty of the Good.* London: Ark Paperbacks.

Myers, G. E. 1986. *William James: His Life and Thought.* New Haven: Yale University Press.

Nabokov, V. 1989. *Speak Memory.* New York: Vintage Books.

Nagel, T. 1986. "Mind." In his *The View from Nowhere.* New York: Oxford University Press.

Nagel, T. 1995. "Searle: Why We Are Not Computers." In his *Other Minds.* New York: Oxford University Press.

Nagel, T. 1998. "Conceiving the impossible and the mind-body problem." *Philosophy* 73 (285): 337–352.

Nauta, W. J. H., and M. Feirtag. 1986. *Fundamental Neuroanatomy.* New York: W. H. Freeman.

Ogden, T. 1994. *Subjects of Analysis.* Northvale, N.J.: Jason Aronson.

Ornston, D. 1985. "The invention of 'cathexis' and Strachey's strategy." *International Review of Psycho-analysis* 12: 391–398.

Ozick, C. 1991. *Metaphor and Memory.* New York: Vintage International.

Pally, R. 1997. "Memory: brain systems that link past, present, and future." *International Journal of Psychoanalysis* 78 (6): 1223–1234.

Panksepp, J. 1998a. *Affective Neuroscience.* New York: Oxford University Press.

Panksepp, J. 1998b. "The periconscious substrates of consciousness: affective states and the evolutionary origin of the SELF." *Journal of Consciousness Studies* 5: 566–582.

Panksepp, J. 2000. "The neurodynamics of emotions." In *Emotion, Development, and Self-Organization,* edited by M. D. Lewis and I. Granic. Cambridge: Cambridge University Press.

Panksepp, J., and J. Burgdorf. 2000. "50-kHz chirping (laughter?) in response to conditioned and unconditioned tickle-induced reward in rats: effects of social housing and genetic variables." *Behavioral Brain Research* 115: 25–38.

Pantin, C. F. A. 1968. *The Relations between the Sciences.* Cambridge: Cambridge University Press.

Peirce, C. S. 1891. "The architecture of theories." In *Charles S. Peirce: Selected Writings,* edited by P. P. Wiener. New York: Dover Publications.

Peirce, C. A. 1910. "Logic as semiotic: the theory of signs. In *Philosophical Writings of Peirce,* edited by J. Buchler. New York: Dover Publications.

Penrose, R. 1989. *The Emperor's New Mind.* New York: Oxford University Press.

Person, E. S. 1995. *By Force of Fantasy.* New York: Penguin Books.

Piaget, J. 1954. *The Construction of Reality in the Child.* New York: Basic Books.

Pinker, S. 1997. *How the Mind Works.* New York: W. W. Norton.

Plato. 1928. *The Philosophy of Plato*. Edited by Irwin Edman. New York: Modern Library.

Prager, J. 1998. *Presenting the Past*. Cambridge: Harvard University Press.

Pribram, K., and M. Gill. 1976. *Freud's "Project" Re-assessed*. New York: Basic.

Prigogine, I. 1997. *The End of Certainty*. New York: Free Press.

Putnam, H. 1988. *Representation and Reality*. Cambridge: MIT Press.

Putnam, H. 1990. "The craving for objectivity." *Realism with a human face*. J. Conant. Cambridge: Harvard University Press.

Putnam, H. 1997. "James' theory of truth." In *The Cambridge Companion to William James*, edited by R. A. Putnam. Cambridge: Cambridge University Press.

Putnam, H. 1999. *The Threefold Cord: Mind, Body, and World*. New York: Columbia University Press.

Racker, H. 1968. *Transference and Countertransference*. New York: International Universities Press.

Ramachandran, V. S., and D. Blakeslee. 1998. *Phantoms in the Brain*. New York: William Morrow.

Rand, N., and M. Torok. 1997. *Questions for Freud*. Cambridge: Harvard University Press.

Revonsuo, A. 2001. "Can functional brain imaging discover consciousness in the brain?" *Journal of Consciousness Studies* 8 (3): 3–23.

Richards, I. A. 1969. *Coleridge on Imagination*. Bloomington: Indiana University Press.

Rizzolatti, G., and M. Arbib. 1998. "Language within our grasp." *Trends in Neuroscience* 21: 180–194.

Roudinesco, E. 1997. *Jacques Lacan*. New York: Columbia University Press.

Rycroft, C. 1996. *The Innocence of Dreams*. Northvale, N.J.: Jason Aronson.

Sacks, O. 1990. "Neurology and the soul." *New York Review of Books* 37 (18): 44–50.

Sacks, O. 1995. *An Anthropologist on Mars*. New York: Alfred A. Knopf.

Savage-Rumbaugh, S., W. Fields, et al. 2001. "Language, speech tools, and writing: a cultural imperative." *Journal of Consciousness Studies* 8 (5–7): 273–293.

Savage-Rumbaugh, S., and R. Lewin. 1994. *Kanzi.* New York: John Wiley and Sons.

Scarry, E. 1985. *The Body in Pain.* New York: Oxford University Press.

Scarry, E. 1999. *Dreaming by the Book.* New York: Farrar, Straus, Giroux.

Schactel, E. G. 1959. *Metamorphosis.* New York: Basic Books.

Schacter, D. 1996. *Searching for Memory.* New York: Basic Books.

Scheff, T. J. 2000. "Multipersonal dialogues in consciousness: an incident in Virginia Woolf's 'To the Lighthouse'." *Journal of Consciousness Studies* 7 (6): 3–19.

Schilder, P. 1935. *The Image and Appearance of the Human Body.* New York: International Universities Press.

Schore, A. N. 1994. *Affect Regulation and the Origin of the Self.* Hillside, N.J.: Lawrence Erlbaum.

Schwartz, S. 2001. "Camera work." *New York Review of Books* 48 (May 31, 2001): 6–12.

Searle, J. R. 1983. *Intentionality.* Cambridge: Cambridge University Press.

Searle, J. R. 1992. *The Rediscovery of the Mind.* Cambridge: MIT Press.

Searle, J. R. 1997. *The Mystery of Consciousness.* New York: New York Review.

Searle, J. R. 2000. "Consciousness, free action, and the brain." *Journal of Consciousness Studies* 7 (10): 3–22.

Segal, H. 1957. "Notes on symbol formation." *International Journal of Psychoanalysis* 38: 39–45.

Sharpe, E. F. 1940. "Psycho-physical problems revealed in language: an examination of metaphor." In her *Collected Papers on Psycho-analysis.* London: Hogarth Press.

Sheets-Johnstone, M. 1984. *The Roots of Thinking.* Philadelphia: Temple University Press.

Sherrington, C. 1940. *Man on His Nature.* New York: Mentor.

Smuts, B. 2001. "Encounters with animal minds." *Journal of Consciousness Studies* 8 (5–7): 293–309.

Solms, M. 1997a. *The Neuropsychology of Dreams.* Mahwah, N.J.: Lawrence Erlbaum.

Solms, M. 1997b. "What is consciousness?" *Journal of the American Psychoanalytic Association* 45 (3): 681–703.

Solms, M. 1999. "Commentary on the new neuropsychology of sleep." *Neuro-psychoanalysis* 1: 183–195.

Solms, M., and E. Nersessian. 1999. "Freud's theory of affects: questions for neuroscience." *Neuro-psychoanalysis* 1: 5–14.

Spillius, E. B. 2001. "Freud and Klein on the concept of fantasy." *International Journal of Psycho-analysis* 82 (2): 361–373.

Spinoza, B. de. 1675. *A Spinoza Reader.* Princeton: Princeton University Press.

Stern, D. 1985. *The Interpersonal World of the Infant.* New York: Basic Books.

Stern, D. 1994. "One way to build a clinically relevant baby." *Infant Mental Health Journal* 15 (1): 9–25.

Stern, D. 1995. *The Motherhood Constellation.* New York: Basic Books.

Stern, D., N. Bruschweiler-Stern, et al. 1998. "The process of therapeutic change involving implicit knowledge: some implications of developmental observations for adult psychotherapy." *Infant Mental Health Journal* 19 (3): 300–307.

Thelen, E., and L. Smith. 1994. *A Dynamic Systems Approach to the Development of Cognition and Action.* Cambridge: MIT Press.

Thompson, E. 2001. "Between ourselves." *Journal of Consciousness Studies* 8 (5–7).

Todorov, T. 1984. *Mikhail Bakhtin: The Dialogical Principle.* Minneapolis: University of Minnesota Press.

Tomasello, M. 1999. *Human Cognition.* Cambridge: Harvard University Press.

Tononi, G., and G. M. Edelman. 1998. "Consciousness and complexity." *Science* 282: 1846–1851.

Tooby, J., and L. Cosmides. 1990. "The past explains the present." *Ethology and Sociobiology* 11: 375–424.

Toulmin, S. 1990. *Cosmopolis*. Chicago: University of Chicago Press.

Trevarthen, C. 1989. "Intuitive emotions: their changing role in communication between mother and infant." In *Affeti: natura e sviluppo delle relazione interpersonali*, edited by M. Ammaniti. Bari, Italy: Laterza.

Tucker, D. M., and P. Luu. 1998. "Cathexis revisited." In *Neurosciences of the Mind on the Centennial of Freud's Project for a Scientific Psychology*, edited by R. Bilder and F. F. Lefever. New York: New York Academy of Sciences.

Tulving, E. 1972. "Episodic and semantic memory." In *Organization of Memory*, edited by E. Tulving and W. Donaldson. New York: Academic Press.

Turner, M. 1991. *Reading Minds*. Princeton: Princeton University Press.

Turner, M. 1992. "Design for a theory of meaning." In *The Nature and Ontogenesis of meaning*, edited by W. Overton and D. Palermo. Hillside, N.J.: Lawrence Erlbaum Associates.

Varela, F. 1999. "Present-time consciousness." *Journal of Consciousness Studies* 6 (Feb./Mar.): 111–140.

Varela, F., and J. Shear. 1999. "First-person methodologies: what, why, how?" *Journal of Consciousness Studies* 6 (Feb./Mar.): 1–14.

Vargha-Khadem, F., D. G. Gadian, et al. 1997. "Differential effects of early hippocampal pathology on episodic and semantic memory." *Science* 277: 376–380.

Velmans, M. 2000. *Understanding Consciousness*. London: Routledge.

Vico, G. 1744. *The New Science*. Ithaca: Cornell University Press.

Warburg, A. 1995. *Images from the Region of the Pueblo Indians of North America*. Ithaca: Cornell University Press.

Weinberg, S. 2001. "Can science explain everything? Anything?" *New York Review of Books* 48 (9): 47–50.

Weiss, J., and H. Sampson. 1986. *The Psychoanalytic Process*. New York: Guilford Press.

Werbos, P. J. 1993. "Quantum theory and neural systems: alternative approaches and a new design." In *Rethinking neural networks: quantum fields and biological data*, edited by K. H. Pribram. Hillsdale, N.J.: Lawrence Erlbaum Associates.

Whyte, L. L. 1962. *The Unconscious before Freud*. New York: Doubleday.

Wilson, E. O. 1998. *Consilience*. New York: Alfred A. Knopf.

Winnicott, D. 1963. "Communicating and not communicating leading to a study in certain opposites. In his *The Maturational Processes and the Facilitating Environment*. New York: International Universities Press.

Winnicott, D. W. 1971. *Therapeutic Consultations in Child Psychiatry*. New York: Basic Books.

Wolf, N., M. Gales, et al. 2001. "The developmental trajectory from amodal perception to empathy and communication: the role of mirror neurons in this process." *Psychoanalytic Inquiry* 21 (1): 94–112.

Wood, J. 2000. "Eyes wide shut." *New Republic* 441 (4): 27–32.

Wrangham, R. W., W. C. McGrew, et al. 1994. *Chimpanzee Cultures*. Cambridge: Harvard University Press.

Zeki, S. 1993. *A Vision of the Brain*. Oxford: Blackwell.

Zeki, S. 1999. *Inner Vision*. New York: Oxford University Press.

Zimmer, C. 2000. "In search of vertebrate origins: beyond brain and bone." *Science* 287 (5458): 1576–1579.

Index